MAXnotes®

S0-DRW-470

Amy Tan's

The Joy Luck Club

Text by
Carla J. Beard
(M.A. Ball State University)
English Department
Connersville High School
Connersville, Indiana

Illustrations by
Ann Tango-Schurmann

Research & Education Association

MAXnotes® for
THE JOY LUCK CLUB

Printed in the United States of America

Library of Congress Catalog Card Number 96-67452

International Standard Book Number 0-87891-024-7

MAXnotes® is a registered trademark of
Research & Education Association, Piscataway, New Jersey 08854

What **MAXnotes**® *Will Do for You*

This book is intended to help you absorb the essential contents and features of Amy Tan's *The Joy Luck Club* and to help you gain a thorough understanding of the work. The book has been designed to do this more quickly and effectively than any other study guide.

For best results, this **MAXnotes** book should be used as a companion to the actual work, not instead of it. The interaction between the two will greatly benefit you.

To help you in your studies, this book presents the most up-to-date interpretations of every section of the actual work, followed by questions and fully explained answers that will enable you to analyze the material critically. The questions also will help you to test your understanding of the work and will prepare you for discussions and exams.

Meaningful illustrations are included to further enhance your understanding and enjoyment of the literary work. The illustrations are designed to place you into the mood and spirit of the work's settings.

The **MAXnotes** also include summaries, character lists, explanations of plot, and section-by-section analyses. A biography of the author and discussion of the work's historical context will help you put this literary piece into the proper perspective of what is taking place.

The use of this study guide will save you the hours of preparation time that would ordinarily be required to arrive at a complete grasp of this work of literature. You will be well prepared for classroom discussions, homework, and exams. The guidelines that are included for writing papers and reports on various topics will prepare you for any added work which may be assigned.

The **MAXnotes** will take your grades "to the max."

Dr. Max Fogiel
Program Director

Contents

> **Each story includes List of Characters,
> Summary, Analysis, Study Questions and
> Answers, and Suggested Essay Topics.**

Introduction

The Life and Work of Amy Tan

Amy Tan's grandmother, Jing-mei, was widowed when her daughter Daisy was young. She was later forced to marry a wealthy man who had raped her. Since Chinese custom prohibited widows from remarrying, both Jing-mei and Daisy were shunned. Jing-mei eventually committed suicide by eating food with raw opium in it. Daisy later married a man who abused her. She divorced him and came to America, but he forced her to leave their three daughters behind.

In California she met John Tan, an electrical engineer and Baptist minister who had also fled China in the late 1940s. They married soon afterwards. Amy, their second child and only daughter, was born in 1952. Her Chinese name, An-mei, means "gift from America."

Amy Tan said her parents "wanted us to have American circumstances and Chinese character" (*Current Biography,* 560). However, in order to assimilate, the children felt forced to choose "American" ways and to refuse "Chinese" things. This led to a deep sense of "shame and self-hate," Tan said (*Current Biography,* 560). For example, she once wanted to change her Chinese features so much that she went to bed with a clothespin on her nose every night for a week.

After the deaths of her father and older brother, eight months apart, the family spent a year in Europe. Tan was 16 years old. She finished high school early; when her family returned to America, she began college. There she met Louis DeMattei, her future husband, who is now a tax attorney.

Daisy Tan was unhappy when her daughter not only transferred schools to be with DeMattei, but also changed from pre-med to studying English and linguistics. The two did not speak for about six months. Amy Tan completed both her B.A. and M.A. degrees and was working on a doctorate when she left school to work with retarded and developmentally disabled people. Later she started a successful free-lance nonfiction writing business, partly in response to a supervisor who severely criticized her writing. When she and her husband bought Daisy Tan a place to live, Daisy conceded that perhaps writing was a good career for her daughter.

In 1987 Amy Tan went to China with her mother to meet her half-sisters, whom she did not know about until she was 26 ("Mother With a Past," 47). Tan said later, "There was something about this country that I belonged to. I found something about myself that I never knew was there" (*Current Biography*, 561).

Her first short story, "Endgame," was published in 1985 and was followed by "Waiting Between the Trees." When she learned that publishers were interested in the outline for *The Joy Luck Club*, originally titled *Wind and Water*, she left her free-lance business and finished the novel in four months. It was followed by *The Kitchen God's Wife* in 1991 and *The Moon Lady*, a collaboration with Gretchen Schields, in 1992. She also worked on the movie screenplay of *The Joy Luck Club*, released in 1993.

Historical Background

The Japanese invasion of China, part of World War II, began in 1937 and continued until 1945. The Japanese committed atrocities against Chinese prisoners for which they would apologize as late as the 1980s. Many Chinese people fled their homes as the Japanese approached; many died.

After World War II, civil war broke out between the Kuomintang (Nationalist Chinese) under Chiang Kai-shek and the Communists under Mao Zedong and Chou En-lai. During this war as well, many Chinese people fled, either in disagreement with Communism or rightly fearing reprisals. The war ended with Communist victory in 1949. The Nationalist government of Chiang Kai-shek on Formosa (later Taiwan) was recognized as the official Chinese government by the United Nations and most of the Western world. Official diplomatic and trade relations between Communist China (The People's Republic of China) and the United States were severed.

In 1971 the United Nations formally recognized mainland China, and in 1972 American president Richard Nixon visited China and met with Chairman Mao Zedong. Diplomatic relations began on a limited basis. In 1979 the two countries normalized their relationship.

American pop culture during the 1960s and 1970s was affected by events both at home and abroad. Bobby Fischer, a chess Grand Master, angered feminists by claiming that a woman would never be a Grand Master of chess. *Life*, a weekly news magazine with strong emphasis on photography, saw its sales decline, replaced by the immediacy of television. "The Ed Sullivan Show" was a Sunday-night variety program featuring quality acts of everything from opera to plate spinning. Overshadowing everything, the unpopularity of the Vietnam War tore at the unity of families, communities, and the nation.

San Francisco in 1987 was an energetic mix of cultures and lifestyles. Many Americans of minority descent increasingly claimed their ethnic heritage as part of their identity, resisting assimilation. Women sought equal status with men in the workplace, working in such nontraditional fields as tax law. The city was also well known for its substantial gay community, seriously affected by the discovery of AIDS in 1981. Minimalism, an artistic movement marked by spareness, was popular. Self-employment via freelance work was very common, as workers sought alternatives to working for large corporations such as Price, Waterhouse.

Released in March 1989, *The Joy Luck Club* remained on the *New York Times* bestseller list from April through November, an incredible success for a first novel. Critics often compared this novel to Maxine Hong Kingston's autobiography *The Woman Warrior*, because both are about Chinese-American women. They praised Tan's telling detail, skill with dialogue, and empathy for her characters. A few, notably Rhoda Koenig, have suggested that some of the stories resolve themselves too easily and that there may be too much intrusion from Tan's personal life into some events of the novel, especially her reunion with her half-sisters. Most acknowledge, however, that one strength of Tan's novel is its universal themes and common issues among mothers, daughters, and families. Anyone who has a mother will find her in this novel somewhere.

Feminist critic Marina Heung points out that this novel is noteworthy for its inclusion of mothers as subjects and women in their own right, rather than as objects their daughters revolt against (Heung, 598-99). Other critics point to the segmented narrative technique that encourages readers to "think simultaneously in different directions" (Miner, 567), avoiding traditional Western linear thought. These strengths emphasize the novel's importance outside of its ethnic significance.

Master List of Characters

Suyuan Woo—*founder of the Joy Luck Club, mother of Jing-mei (June) Woo and wife of Canning Woo. She dies two months before the novel begins. Her name means "Long-Cherished Wish."*

Jing-mei (June) Woo—*age 36, daughter of Suyuan and Canning Woo. One of the narrators. Her name means "Pure Essence, Younger Sister."*

Canning Woo—*Suyuan's second husband and Jing-mei's (June's) father. He narrates part of one story.*

Mei Han and Mei Ching—*couple who adopt the abandoned daughters of Suyuan.*

Wang Chwun Yu and Wang Chwun Hwa—*twin daughters of Suyuan and her first husband, half sisters of Jing-mei Woo. Their names mean "Spring Rain" and "Spring Flower."*

Aiyi—*aunt of Canning Woo, great-aunt of Jing-mei.*

Lili—*Aiyi's great-granddaughter.*

Mr. Chong (Old Chong)—*Jing-mei's deaf piano teacher.*

An-mei Hsu—*friend of Suyuan, wife of George and mother of Rose, Ruth, Janice, Matthew, Mark, Luke, and Bing. One of the narrators.*

George Hsu—*An-mei's husband, Rose's father.*

Bing Hsu—*One of An-mei's children, he drowns. His name means "Good Fortune."*

An-mei's mother—*never named, she was disowned by her family because she married Wu Tsing. She commits suicide.*

Popo—*An-mei's maternal grandmother. She dies of an illness.*

An-mei's brother—*never named, he is younger than An-mei. After Popo's death he remains with Auntie and Uncle.*

Uncle and Auntie—*An-mei's mother's brother and his wife. Popo and the children live with them.*

Wu Tsing—*second husband of An-mei's mother. A rich merchant who raped her.*

Rose Hsu Jordan—*daughter of An-mei and George Hsu, wife of Ted Jordan. One of the narrators.*

Ted Jordan—*Rose's husband, a dermatologist.*

Mrs. Jordan—*Ted's mother. She tries to prevent Rose and Ted from seeing each other.*

Old Mr. Chou—*Chinese equivalent of the Sandman.*

Yan Chang—*An-mei's mother's servant.*

First Wife—*Wu Tsing's wife. She has two daughters and is addicted to opium.*

Second Wife—*Wu Tsing's first concubine. She dominates the household through manipulation.*

Third Wife—*another of Wu Tsing's concubines. She is the mother of three daughters.*

Fifth Wife—*Wu Tsing's newest concubine. She is young and from a poor family.*

Syaudi—*son of Wu Tsing and An-mei's mother, An-mei's half brother. Second Wife claims him as her own.*

Lindo's helper in Peking—*never named, she gives Lindo advice about coming to America.*

Lindo's helper in San Francisco—*never named, she helps Lindo get an apartment and a job.*

Lindo Jong—*friend of Suyuan, wife of Tin and mother of Winston, Vincent, and Waverly. In China she was married to Tyan-yu. One of the narrators.*

Tin Jong—*Lindo's second husband, Waverly's father.*

Winston and Vincent Jong—*sons of Lindo and Tin.*

Waverly Jong—*daughter of Lindo and Tin. One of the narrators.*

Shoshana—*Waverly's daughter from her first marriage.*

Lindo's mother—*never named.*

The Matchmaker—*arranges the marriage of Lindo and Tyan-yu.*

The Matchmaker's Assistant—*she inadvertently makes possible a divorce of Lindo and Tyan-yu without disgrace to Lindo.*

The Servant Girl—*very kind to Lindo. Lindo arranges for her to marry Tyan-yu.*

Tyan-yu—*Lindo's first husband. His name means "Sky Leftovers."*

Huang Taitai—*Lindo's first mother-in-law, mother of Tyan-yu.*

Mr. Rory—*Waverly's hairdresser.*

Marvin Chen—*Waverly's first husband, Shoshana's father.*

Lau Po—*an old man in the park who teaches Waverly chess.*

Rich Schields—*engaged to Waverly, a tax attorney.*

Ying-ying St. Clair—*mother of Lena, wife of Clifford St. Clair. One of the narrators. Her name means "Clear Reflection."*

Clifford St. Clair—*husband of Ying-ying, whom he calls "Betty," and father of Lena.*

Lena St. Clair—*daughter of Ying-ying and Clifford St. Clair, wife of Harold Livotny. One of the narrators.*

Ying-ying's first husband—*never named. He is murdered by a mistress.*

Amah—*Ying-ying's nanny.*

Chang-o—*the Moon Lady, a character from Chinese mythology.*

Syi Wang Mu, Queen Mother of the Western Skies—*a character from Chinese mythology.*

Hou Yi, Master Archer of the Skies—*husband of Chang-o, a character from Chinese mythology.*

Number Two and Number Three—*Ying-ying's younger sisters.*

Mama and Baba—*Ying-ying's parents.*

Teresa Sorci—*a girl about two years older than Lena who lives next door in their apartment building.*

Harold Livotny—*Lena's husband, a restaurant designer and developer.*

Arnold—*a neighbor who was mean to Lena when they were children.*

Summary of the Novel

The novel contains four sections, each beginning with a vignette depicting a stage in the life cycle. The four stories in each section explore the relationship between the mothers and the daughters at the same stage.

One series of stories focuses on Suyuan Woo, who comes to America in 1947, having lost her family, including twin daughters, during war. She does not know her daughters were rescued. Now remarried, she settles in San Francisco, has a daughter, Jing-mei (June), and starts a Joy Luck Club similar to one in China with three other women. The four form strong friendships.

As she grows up, Jing-mei and her mother struggle to understand one another. They never completely resolve their differences, and Suyuan dies unexpectedly. At the next meeting of the Joy Luck Club, her mother's friends tell Jing-mei that Suyuan's twin daughters have been found. They give her a check so she can visit them. As the novel ends, she meets her sisters in Shanghai.

A second set of stories focuses on An-mei, who lives with her grandmother because her mother has been disowned. When An-mei is nine, her grandmother dies; and An-mei leaves with her mother to live in the home of a wealthy man and his other wives. An-mei learns how her mother was forced into a dishonorable second marriage and why she has no control over her own life. Her mother's subsequent suicide provides An-mei a better life.

As an adult An-mei comes to San Francisco. She and her husband have seven children, including Rose. Rose marries Ted, a dermatologist, who has an affair and divorces her. Rose is overwhelmed but recovers.

The third series of stories focuses on Lindo. She marries Tyan-yu, but he never sleeps with her. Unable to tell her domineering mother-in-law the truth, she devises a clever plan and is released from her marriage honorably. She comes to San Francisco and marries Tin Jong. They have three children—Winston, Vincent, and Waverly.

Waverly is a child chess prodigy. She and her mother maneuver through their differences throughout her childhood and into adulthood. Their differences climax over Waverly's fiancé, Rich Schields, and the two women reconcile.

The fourth series of stories focuses on Ying-ying. Born into a wealthy family, she is a spirited child who nearly drowns when she is four. She grows into a haughty young woman and marries a crude man who abandons her after she becomes pregnant. Ten years later she marries Clifford St. Clair, an American exporter, even though she doesn't love him. They come to San Francisco and have one daughter, Lena. Their second child is stillborn, and Ying-ying is depressed for months afterward. Her depression affects Lena.

As an adult Lena marries Harold Livotny, who takes advantage of her. Ying-ying feels responsible for raising so powerless a daughter. She wants to encourage Lena to speak up for herself.

Estimated Reading Time

The novel consists of 16 short stories, each requiring 25 to 40 minutes to read, and four vignettes requiring five minutes each to read. The entire novel can be completed in about 10 to 11 hours.

The Joy Luck Club

Feathers from a Thousand Li Away

Vignette

Summary

A young woman leaves China to come to America. She brings with her a swan she plans to give to the daughter she will have someday, a daughter whose life will be much better than hers. Once they arrive in America, though, immigration officials take the swan away from her, leaving her only a feather.

As the vignette concludes, the woman has grown old. She has a daughter but has never given her the feather because she wants to be able to explain her "good intentions" in "perfect American English."

Analysis

This vignette focuses on the mother's actions when she was young and their effects later. Both the woman and the daughter are archetypes, or patterns, of the characters in the rest of the novel. Readers often try to identify the woman in the vignette as Suyuan,

the mother in the next story, but she is not. The four stories in this section also focus on the mothers when they were young. As the novel progresses, the reader will see these events affect both mother and daughter later.

The swan is a symbol of the mother. In the first paragraph, the vendor says the swan was "a duck that stretched its neck"; in the second paragraph both swan and mother "[stretch] their necks toward America." The swan is described as "a creature that became more than what was hoped for," suggesting that the mother's life in America will be better than she had hoped for in China. When immigration officials confiscate the swan, Tan describes the mother as "fluttering her arms" like flapping wings.

The feather represents the mother's "good intentions." She wants to give her daughter part of herself, but she hesitates, waiting until she can explain herself "in perfect American English." The fact that the woman is now old suggests that day will never come, the explanation will never be given, and the daughter will never understand exactly what her mother intended.

The giving of gifts forms a motif throughout this novel. As you read, pay attention to how often gifts are given and whether they are appreciated.

Study Questions

1. Where had the woman purchased the swan?

2. According to the market vendor, what was the swan originally?

3. What is a *li*?

4. How was a woman's value determined in China?

5. What are three hopes the woman has for the daughter she dreams of?

6. Why doesn't the woman have the swan any more?

7. Why has the woman forgotten "why she had come and what she had left behind"?

8. What symbol represents the woman's good intentions?

9. To whom does the woman wish to give this symbol?

10. Why hasn't she done so?

Answers

1. She purchased it in the market in Shanghai.

2. The swan was a duck that tried to become a goose and became a swan instead, "too beautiful to eat."

3. A *li* is about one-third of a mile.

4. If her husband belched loudly, it meant he had eaten a great deal, presumably because his wife was a good cook. Her ability to meet his needs determined her value.

5. First, her daughter will be valued for who she is. Second, she will speak perfect English, suggesting a good education, and no one will look down on her. Third, she will be happy, "too full to swallow any sorrow!"

6. The immigration officials took it away.

7. She had to fill out too many forms; she was caught up in routine activities.

8. The swan feather symbolizes her good intentions.

9. She wants to give it to her daughter.

10. The mother wants to be able to explain herself "in perfect American English."

Suggested Essay Topics

1. In what ways might this mother represent all immigrants to America?

2. In what ways might this mother represent all parents?

The Joy Luck Club

New Characters:

Jing-mei (June) Woo: *narrator of most of this story; age 36, daughter of Suyuan and Canning Woo*

Suyuan Woo: *narrator of part of the story; Jing-mei's mother, Canning Woo's wife, and founder of the Joy Luck Club. She dies two months before the story begins*

Canning Woo: *Suyuan's husband; Jing-mei's father*

An-mei Hsu: *Suyuan's friend; one of the members of the Joy Luck Club*

George Hsu: *An-mei's husband*

Lindo Jong: *Suyuan's "best friend and arch rival"; one of the members of the Joy Luck Club*

Ying-ying St. Clair: *Suyuan's friend; one of the members of the Joy Luck Club*

Uncle Jack: *Ying-ying's younger brother*

Waverly Jong: *Lindo's daughter, one month younger than Jing-mei*

Lena St. Clair: *Ying-ying's daughter*

Summary

Jing-mei, the narrator, attends a meeting of the Joy Luck Club to replace her mother, who has died two months earlier. The story flashes back to Suyuan and Canning Woo's arrival in San Francisco. Suyuan invites three other women to start the Joy Luck Club. As Jing-mei remembers what her mother told her about the first Joy Luck Club, in China, the story shifts, and Suyuan becomes the narrator.

Suyuan's first husband, an officer in the Kuomintang, had sent her and their twin daughters to Kweilin to escape the invading Japanese. To fight misery and despair, she started the Joy Luck Club with three other women. One morning an army officer warned her the Japanese were about to invade. She packed her daughters and some household belongings into a stolen wheelbarrow and fled on foot. When she arrived in Chungking, however, she had only

the clothes she wore. When Jing-mei asks what happened to the babies, Suyuan says only, "Your father is not my first husband. You are not those babies."

The story returns to the American Joy Luck Club, now a successful stock investment club. After eating, the women play mah jong, with Jing-mei taking her mother's place. While they play, the aunties gossip and talk about their children.

When Jing-mei rises to leave, the aunties ask her to stay. Ying-ying tells her Suyuan had never given up hope of finding her twin daughters. Just after her death, someone found them. The aunties give Jing-mei a check for $1,200 and tell her to visit her sisters and tell them about her mother. Jing-mei protests that she doesn't know what to tell them. The aunties, incredulous, point out different facets of Suyuan she can talk about.

Jing-mei suddenly understands that they are afraid their own daughters also don't know anything about them. She says, "I will remember everything about her and tell them." Doubtful but hopeful, they return to telling stories, leaving Jing-mei sitting at the mah jong table, "on the East, where things begin."

Analysis

"The Joy Luck Club" is the title of both the novel and this story. Author Amy Tan introduces and explains the concept of "joy luck" by showing two different Joy Luck Clubs in action.

The first Joy Luck Club, in Kweilin, shielded the women's spirits against the harsh living conditions and constant threat of war. Suyuan had dreamed of visiting Kweilin, a place of great natural beauty, where she thought she would be perfectly happy. Instead, she and the other refugees lived with bad food, disease, over-crowding, and uncertainty. To combat their fear, the women played mah jong once a week. "Each week we could hope to be lucky. That hope was our only joy. And that's how we came to call our little parties Joy Luck."

The second Joy Luck Club, in San Francisco, offered hope to women with a common bond. Jing-mei says:

> My mother could sense that the women of these families also had unspeakable tragedies they had left behind in China and hopes they couldn't begin to express in their fragile English.

The second Joy Luck Club becomes an investment group and social gathering by the time Jing-mei is an adult, and the women have formed strong friendships.

"Joy luck" has become a concept the women would like to pass on to their American-born daughters, who do not understand the tragedies their mothers experienced. The mothers are afraid they will have "grandchildren born without any connecting hope passed from generation to generation."

Tan uses the device of the Joy Luck Club meeting to introduce the mothers and the daughters. She offers initial insight into the mothers' characters by giving Suyuan's opinion of them and develops the characters of Jing-mei (June) and Suyuan.

The conversation about black sesame-seed soup in the first few paragraphs reveals that Jing-mei understands some Chinese, but imperfectly. Her statement, "I can never remember things I didn't understand in the first place," begins the development of two conflicts. In the first, Jing-mei struggles with understanding her Chinese heritage. Not until the final pages does she come to terms with it. The second conflict, overcoming language problems, affects all the characters to greater and lesser degrees. Later in the story, Jing-mei states she felt as though "my mother and I spoke two different languages, which we did. I talked to her in English, she answered back in Chinese." Mothers and daughters struggle with their imperfect understandings of one another, seeking reconciliation.

Suyuan is a complex character. She has built such strong friendships with An-mei, Lindo, and Ying-ying that they are willing to pay for Jing-mei to visit China and see Suyuan's daughters. However, Suyuan was also very critical of them. She claimed An-mei had no spine and never thought about what she was doing; she competed with Lindo by comparing their daughters; and she said Ying-ying was not hard of hearing but "hard of listening." This criticism of her best friends suggests she is able to see and appreciate someone beyond her flaws. The reader will see her apply this appreciation to her own daughter as the novel progresses.

This story also introduces a continuing motif, the idea of seeking balance. Suyuan's criticism runs along the lines of "Something was always missing. Something always needed improving. Something was not in balance." Auntie Lindo explains that Jing-mei will take her mother's place at mah jong because without her the women are "like a table with three legs, no balance." These are minor examples of what will be a significant concept in the novel.

Study Questions

1. Why did Suyuan organize the first Joy Luck Club?

2. What are *dyansyin* foods?

3. According to Suyuan's story, what happened to her twin daughters?

4. With whom did Suyuan compare Jing-mei?

5. According to Suyuan, what is the difference between Jewish and Chinese mah jong?

6. Auntie An-mei had gone to China "three years ago," according to the story. Tell at least two things that went wrong on the trip.

7. What motivates the aunties to give Jing-mei money for a trip to China?

8. What do the aunties want Jing-mei to tell her sisters in China about?

9. Jing-mei comments on the English of her mother and the other members of the Joy Luck Club, calling it "halting" and "fractured." How does this relate to the old woman of the vignette, who wants to speak "perfect American English"? What does it suggest about Suyuan, An-mei, Lindo, and Ying-ying?

10. List four examples of breakdown in communication between Suyuan and Jing-mei.

Answers

1. Suyuan organized the first Joy Luck Club to fight discouragement during the war.

2. *Dyansyin* foods are supposed to bring good luck. They include dumplings shaped like ingots, rice noodles, boiled peanuts, and oranges.

3. Suyuan does not say. We only know that she arrived in Chungking without them.

4. Suyuan compared Jing-mei with Lindo's daughter, Waverly, who was one month younger.

5. In Jewish mah jong, players focus on their own tiles. In Chinese mah jong, players also note what their opponents are playing and use strategy.

6. First, her brother's family was not impressed with her gifts of candy and cheap clothing. Second, they took advantage of her by bringing along extended family members and some people who weren't even related and manipulating her into providing meals and lodging at an expensive hotel for everyone, three gifts for each relative, and a loan that was never repaid.

7. The aunties are generous women who feel a strong loyalty to the friend who brought them together.

8. The aunties want Jing-mei to tell her sisters about their mother. They specifically mention Suyuan's success, her intelligence, kindness, care of her family, hopes, and cooking.

9. Suyuan, An-mei, Lindo, and Ying-ying, as mothers, want their daughters to understand them. However, language problems may get in the way.

10. A) Jing-mei does not remember whether her mother said black sesame-seed soup and red bean soup were *chabudwo*, almost the same, or *butong*, not the same thing at all.

    B) Jing-mei does not understand why her mother was so critical of her own friends.

    C) Suyuan has trouble explaining the difference between Jewish and Chinese mah jong to Jing-mei.

    D) Suyuan told Lindo that Jing-mei was returning to college when Jing-mei had only said she would "look into it" and did not really intend to.

Suggested Essay Topics
1. Compare and contrast Suyuan's expectation of Kweilin with the reality of her life there.

2. Based on the details in this story, describe Suyuan.

3. Based on the details in this story, describe Jing-mei.

Scar

New Characters:

Popo: *An-mei's maternal grandmother. An-mei and her brother have lived with her the last five years*

An-mei's mother: *she is never given a name. Her family has ostracized her because she disgraced them*

An-mei's brother: *younger than An-mei*

Uncle and Auntie: *Popo and the two children live with them in Ningpo, China*

Summary

An-mei, now an old woman, narrates this story. As a child, she and her brother live with Popo, Auntie, and Uncle. As Popo grows increasingly ill, she calls An-mei to her bedside and tells her stories with a moral to them. Both Popo and Auntie tell the children that their mother has no respect for the family. An-mei feels unlucky to have such a mother.

The story jumps ahead to when An-mei is nine, and her mother returns. Auntie, Uncle, and the servants, unhappy with her presence, ignore her. She goes to Popo's room and begins to take care of her. Popo is so sick she doesn't even know who is there. If she had known who it was, she would have thrown An-mei's mother out.

An-mei says her mother's voice confused her, "a familiar sound from a forgotten dream." Later she remembers when she had heard her mother's voice before.

She had been four. During an argument between her mother and the rest of the family, a large pot of hot soup on the dinner table spilled on An-mei's neck. The burn was very serious. The first

night Popo told An-mei the family had made burial clothes for her, her mother had left, and if An-mei did not get well soon, her mother would forget her. An-mei recovered. Two years later the scar on her neck was pale and shiny, and she had completely forgotten her mother.

The story returns to the time when An-mei is nine, and Popo is dying. Her mother repeats an ancient tradition. She cuts a piece of flesh from her arm, puts it into a special soup, and feeds Popo, partly in one last attempt to save her life and partly out of respect for her. Popo dies a few hours later.

An-mei, now in the present, says that even then she could tell how much respect her mother had for Popo: "It is *shou* so deep it is in your bones." Sometimes the only way to remember what is in your bones is to peel off everything until there is nothing else left.

Analysis

At the end of "The Joy Luck Club," when Jing-mei protests that she doesn't know anything about Suyuan, An-mei exclaims, "Your mother is in your bones!" This story shows how she has come to believe this.

"Scar" focuses on *shou*, respect for family. In this important Chinese tradition, respect is granted automatically; it does not have to be earned. The American-born daughters will not view respect for the family in the same manner as their mothers. This difference in the two cultures and generations creates conflict throughout the novel.

An-mei's mother has disgraced her family. An-mei's father died, and Chinese tradition forbids widows to remarry. For reasons we are not told in this story, however, she has remarried. Worse, she married a wealthy man who already had three wives.

Both Popo and Auntie teach An-mei and her brother that their mother is bad. The children think she is "thoughtless" and "a traitor to our ancestors." Eventually An-mei believes them and considers herself unlucky to have such a mother. However, she thinks these thoughts while hiding from the portrait of her father, suggesting that she knew she was being disrespectful.

The story does not tell how An-mei's mother knew Popo was dying. She returns to take care of her mother, even cutting flesh from her own arm for a special soup. She knew she could not save

Popo's life. The important thing was to demonstrate *shou*. An-mei realized that showing respect for Popo did not depend on whether Popo showed respect for her. She saw her mother's sacrifice for Popo as a way of honoring her.

The title of the story, "Scar," can be interpreted three ways. Most obvious is what An-mei calls her "smooth-neck scar," the result of being burned by the soup. A second, an emotional scar, is suggested when An-mei says:

> In two years' time, my scar became pale and shiny and I had no memory of my mother. That is the way it is with a wound. The wound begins to close in on itself, to protect what is hurting so much. And once it is closed, you no longer see what is underneath, what started the pain.

An-mei's mother will have a scar as a result of the wound to her arm in addition to emotional scars from being separated from her children and disowned by her family. In another story we will see that she carries scars from other incidents in her life, too.

Popo is also scarred. From her point of view, disowning her daughter was the right thing to do. Even so, she has suffered. Her daughter is gone, and her family is in disgrace.

Study Questions

1. Who is Popo and how did she affect both An-mei's mother and An-mei herself?

2. How does An-mei describe the house in Ningpo?

3. In what ways does Popo demonstrate that she loves An-mei and her brother?

4. In addition to remarrying, what had An-mei's mother done that indicated a lack of respect for her family?

5. What caused An-mei's smooth-neck scar?

6. Popo recognizes the seriousness of An-mei's injury and tries to give her the will to live. What does she say to An-mei that helps her recover?

7. Why do Popo and Auntie speak badly of An-mei's mother?

8. Why does An-mei's mother return to Uncle and Auntie's house?

9. In what way does An-mei's mother demonstrate "*shou* so deep it is in your bones"?

10. In the last several paragraphs, An-mei makes several references to "what is in your bones." What does she mean?

Answers

1. Popo is An-mei's maternal grandmother. She forced An-mei's mother to leave the house and leave her children behind because she had remarried after her husband's death. She made An-mei feel unlucky to have such a bad mother. She took good care of An-mei in other ways, though, and An-mei knew she loved her.

2. An-mei mentions "cold hallways and tall stairs." She also says "our house was so unhappy." A portrait of her father, "a large, unsmiling man" hangs in the main hall.

3. Popo tries to keep the ghosts from stealing the children. She tells them stories to teach them right from wrong. She takes care of An-mei's burn, including telling her things to give her the will to live. Even her decision to disown An-mei's mother is an effort to do the right thing from her point of view.

4. An-mei's mother had gone to her new home without taking the furniture from her dowry, without taking 10 pairs of silver chopsticks, and without visiting her husband's grave or the other family graves.

5. An-mei's smooth-neck scar is the result of a bad burn. A pot of boiling soup spilled on her when she was four.

6. First Popo tells An-mei that the family is prepared for her death. If she dies, her funeral will be simple and her family will not mourn her very long. Second, and more important to An-mei, Popo tells her that her mother has left and will forget all about her if she dies.

7. Popo and Auntie speak badly of An-mei's mother because she disgraced her family. Instead of remaining a widow, she married a wealthy man who already had three wives; and she left without showing respect to the family ancestors.

8. An-mei's mother returns to Uncle and Auntie's house because Popo is dying. She is the oldest daughter and wants to show respect.

9. An-mei's mother demonstrates *shou* when she makes a soup of herbs and medicines and cuts a piece of flesh from her own arm. Then she feeds the soup to her dying mother, hoping to save her life. She does this even though her mother had disowned her and forced her to leave without her children.

10. By "in your bones" An-mei refers to people's true nature, who they are when stripped of all artificiality.

Suggested Essay Topics

1. What evidence in the story suggests that Popo was a good mother, not only to An-mei and her brother, but also to her daughter, An-mei's mother?

2. What factors might have caused An-mei's mother to leave at the time An-mei needed her most?

3. In what ways are An-mei, her mother, and Popo "scarred"?

The Red Candle

New Characters:

Lindo's mother: *never named*

Huang Taitai: *Lindo's mother-in-law, mother of Tyan-yu*

Tyan-yu: *Lindo's first husband*

The village matchmaker: *she arranges both the match and later, the wedding, between Lindo and Tyan-yu*

The matchmaker's servant: *her mistake gives Lindo a chance to escape her marriage honorably*

Another servant girl: *she works for Huang Taitai and is kind to Lindo. When she becomes pregnant, Lindo helps her*

Summary

Lindo Jong speaks to her daughter, Waverly, about the importance of keeping promises, comparing them to 24-carat gold. Then she talks about the promise her family made when they arranged the marriage between Lindo and Tyan-yu.

When she is 12, flooding destroys her family's farm, forcing them to move away. Lindo moves in with the Huangs, where she is treated like a servant. Determined that Huang Taitai will not be able to say anything against her family, she makes the best of circumstances. For the next four years Tyan-yu goes out of his way to treat her badly, and Huang Taitai makes sure she is thoroughly trained in household chores. When Huang Taitai announces that she is ready to become a grandmother, preparations begin for the wedding.

Just before the ceremony, Lindo cries about being forced into this marriage. Then she notices the wind. She says, "I realized it was the first time I could see the power of the wind." She looks into the mirror and realizes that she is like the wind—strong, pure, and able to think for herself. She promises herself she will respect her parents' wishes but she will also never forget herself.

During the ceremony a red candle is lit at both ends and placed in a special holder. The matchmaker's servant is to make sure neither end goes out. According to Chinese tradition, when the two ends burn together and flicker out, the husband and wife are joined in spirit forever.

After the wedding banquet the couple is escorted to their bedroom. Tyan-yu tells Lindo to sleep on the sofa. After he is asleep, Lindo walks into the courtyard. Through a window she sees the matchmaker's servant sleepily tending the candle. A sudden crack of thunder frightens the servant, and she runs out. Lindo impulsively runs in and blows out her husband's end of the candle. Then she returns to her room.

The next day, the matchmaker announces that the candle had burned from both ends. Lindo notices that her servant seems "shame-faced" and "mournful."

Lindo is a model wife in front of Huang Taitai, but every night she sleeps on the sofa. One morning Huang Taitai slaps her and says she will not feed or clothe Lindo if she refuses to sleep with her son. Lindo understands that Tyan-yu has lied to his mother about why

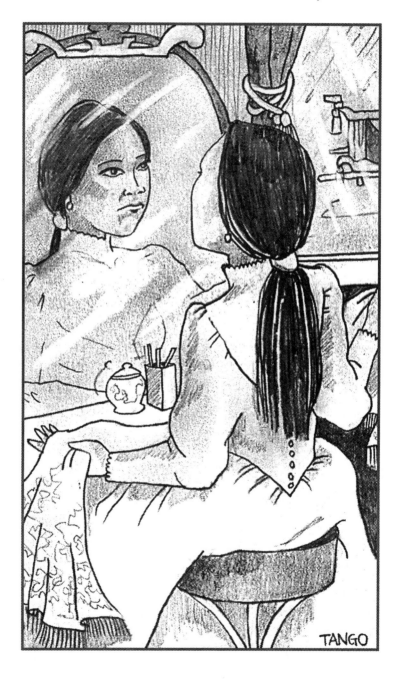

Lindo is not pregnant, and she begins to sleep in the same bed with him. She develops a protective, sisterly feeling toward him.

A few months later Huang Taitai again becomes angry that Lindo is not pregnant and insists that Lindo remain in bed until she is. A servant apologetically serves her a bad-tasting medicine every day. When Lindo still does not become pregnant, the matchmaker is summoned. She announces that Lindo has too much metal, that she is out of balance and cannot conceive. Huang Taitai happily reclaims the jewelry she gave to Lindo as wedding gifts; Lindo begins to plan her escape from this marriage.

Early in the morning on the day of the Festival of Pure Brightness, she cries out, claiming to have a bad dream. She tells everyone the ancestors are angry. They know that the marriage candle did not burn all the way through, as the matchmaker claimed; and they will begin the cycle of destruction if this marriage is not ended. Lindo also says that they have given three signs. First, a mole on Tyan-yu's back will grow and kill him. Second, Lindo's teeth will fall out one at a time. Third, one of the ancestors has impregnated a servant who is Tyan-yu's true spiritual wife.

Huang Taitai finds the mole on Tyan-yu's back and a tooth Lindo had lost four years earlier. Eventually she finds the pregnant servant and learns the truth about the wedding candle from the matchmaker's servant. She releases Lindo from her marriage honorably.

The story ends in the present. Lindo tells Waverly, "I know what I'm worth," as she describes buying 24-carat gold bracelets every few years. She still observes the Festival of Pure Brightness, however, by removing all her jewelry and remembering the promise she made not to forget herself.

Analysis

At the end of "The Joy Luck Club" Jing-mei says that she doesn't know what to tell her half sisters about their mother. Lindo says, "Tell them stories of your family here. How she became success." This story reveals that Lindo knows the meaning of success.

The Huang house serves as a metaphor for the family. Its placement high on a hillside represents their social status. When Lindo says, "they looked down on us," she speaks both literally and figuratively. The river rocks of the house's first level suggest humble origins. Each succeeding level grows more ostentatious until "someone, probably Huang Taitai" adds imperial pretensions. Inside, only the room guests see is lavished with "the look of wealth and old prestige"; the rest of the house is "crowded" and "uncomfortable." Lindo also says the house has "a confused look" to it, a parallel to the confusion she will later manipulate as she convinces Huang Taitai to find another wife for Tyan-yu. This family is only concerned with appearances, foreshadowing their treatment of Lindo and providing her with an essential element of her escape. Their facade is no match for her integrity.

Lindo rescues the pregnant servant from tragedy by claiming she is Tyan-yu's true wife. Pregnancy without marriage was very serious in China; it caused a "loss of face," public embarrassment, not only to the woman and her family, but also to the entire village. History records acts of violence by the village against an unwed mother and her family that could easily result in death. Lindo is apparently the only one who has noticed the servant's condition so far.

She adds a nice touch when she announces that the servant is really of imperial blood. That claim will appeal to Huang Taitai, who will gain status by including her in the family. The servant is astute enough to go along with it; Lindo relates ironically, "they forced her to tell the truth about her imperial ancestry." The servant also cherishes her good fortune. Lindo says she orders the servants to sweep the graves of the ancestors, demonstrating *shou*, once a day instead of the traditional once a year.

Lindo is able to protect Tyan-yu, whom she has come to think of fondly; provide Huang Taitai with a grandson; repay the servant for her kindness; and keep her promises while extricating herself from this abusive situation. That constitutes success by any definition.

Study Questions

1. According to Chinese thinking, what is the difference between 14-carat and 24-carat gold?

2. Lindo relates a movie plot in which a promise is broken. Describe the plot.

3. What qualities would a Chinese mother expect of her daughter-in-law?

4. Describe Lindo as a child.

5. Why does Lindo move in with the Huangs four years before she marries Tyan-yu?

6. What final gift does Lindo's mother give her?

7. What are some ways in which Tyan-yu and Huang Taitai are unkind to Lindo?

8. On her wedding day Lindo compares herself to the wind. In what ways does she say they are alike?

9. How is Lindo able to leave her marriage honorably?

10. Lindo claims the ancestors have given signs that her marriage to Tyan-yu should end. What are the three signs?

Answers

1. The Chinese accept only 24-carat gold, "pure inside and out," as real gold. Fourteen-carat gold isn't gold.

2. In the movie, an American soldier promises to come back and marry a girl he wants to sleep with. She gives in, but he abandons her and later marries another.

3. The mother would expect her daughter-in-law to raise sons, to take care of her husband's parents when they were old, and to show respect to the family ancestors.

4. As a child, Lindo was physically attractive, healthy and strong, and obedient.

5. A flood destroys the farm and home of Lindo's family, forcing them to move to another part of China. Lindo is old enough to stay with the Huangs. She will marry Tyan-yu to fulfill the marriage contract.

6. Lindo's mother gives her a *chang*, a necklace made with a piece of flat red jade.

7. Tyan-yu complains about Lindo's cooking, creates a mess for her to clean up, interrupts her meal with demands to wait on him, and complains about the expression on her face. Huang Taitai criticizes her constantly. She insists that Lindo be trained in how to wash rice, to smell a chamber pot to

make sure it's clean, to do laundry, embroider, and attend to Huang Taitai's personal needs.

8. Both the wind and Lindo have power; both are strong and pure.

9. First, Tyan-yu's end of the marriage candle went out on their wedding night. Second, Lindo made the Huangs think it was their idea for her to leave. Her family would not lose face.

10. The three signs are a mole on Tyan-yu's back, which Lindo claims will grow and eat away his skin; a tooth missing from her own mouth; and a servant who is pregnant with a child who is supposedly Tyan-yu's.

Suggested Essay Topics

1. Is Lindo's behavior in this story consistent with the description given of her in the first story, "The Joy Luck Club"? Explain your answer.

2. Compare and contrast the description of the Huang house with the people who live in it.

The Moon Lady

New Characters:

Amah: *Ying-ying's nanny*

Chang-o, the Moon Lady: *in Chinese tradition, wife of the Master Archer*

Hou Yi, the Master Archer: *husband of Chang-o, associated with the sun*

The Queen Mother of the Western Skies: *also called Syi Wang Mu, associated with the yin principle*

Mama and Baba: *Ying-ying's parents*

Number Two and Number Three: *Ying-ying's younger half sisters*

The family on the fishing boat: *they rescue Ying-ying*

Summary

Ying-ying, the narrator, speaks of her daughter, Lena, who does not hear or see Ying-ying because Ying-ying has kept her "true nature" hidden, "running along like a small shadow so nobody could catch me." She says that both she and Lena are lost, "unseen and not seeing, unheard and not hearing, unknown by others."

The story flashes back to 1918, when Ying-ying is four, and her family is preparing to celebrate the Moon Festival. They have rented a large boat on Tai Lake for the day, and a special ceremony will take place in the evening. Part of the ceremony is when Chang-o, the Moon Lady, grants a secret wish.

Ying-ying chases a dragonfly. Amah becomes upset that Ying-ying's clothes and hair are a mess. Her mother tells her that boys can be active and run, but girls must be still, so the dragonfly will seek their shadow. Ying-ying had not noticed her shadow before; captivated, she plays with it until the family leaves for the lake.

The boat the family has rented is a floating pavilion with elaborate furnishings and decorations. Alone at the back of the boat at sunset, Ying-ying dangles her legs over the side and looks at her reflection. Noticing the large full moon, she twists around to tell the Moon Lady her secret wish and falls into the lake.

By chance a fishing boat catches her in its net. Her rescuers leave her on shore, expecting her family to find her there.

Ying-ying hides in some bushes until she hears music and an announcement that a play dramatizing the Moon Lady's story is about to begin. The Moon Lady in silhouette tells her story from behind a screen that represents the moon. As the play ends, one of the actors tells the audience that the Moon Lady will grant one secret wish to each person for a small fee. The audience breaks up, and no one notices Ying-ying leave the bushes and run forward with her wish.

She runs all the way to the other side to talk to the Moon Lady, who has left the stage. The actor removes both costume and wig, and Ying-ying sees, just as she is stating her wish, that the Moon Lady is a man.

The story returns to the present, and Ying-ying says that for many years she couldn't remember what she wished for that night or how her family found her. She is certain that the entire

experience changed her. But as she has grown older, some of the memories of the day have returned, and today, once again the Moon Festival, she has finally remembered her wish: to be found.

Analysis

In "The Joy Luck Club," when Jing-mei states she won't know what to tell her half sisters about their mother, Ying-ying suggests telling them "what you know about her mind that has become your mind." The theme of the mother's way of thinking strongly influencing the daughter's way of thinking is suggested at the beginning of this story; it becomes quite striking when all four of the stories about Ying-ying are put together. In this first story we see most clearly two motifs and the initial development of Ying-ying's character.

The first motif, alluded to in "The Joy Luck Club," is the Daoist concept of seeking balance: the yin and the yang. This motif dominates the novel. The Moon Lady sadly states, "For woman is yin, the darkness within, where untempered passions lie. And man is yang, bright truth lighting our minds." The yin, or female principle, refers to emotion, passivity, chaos, wetness, and the body; the yang, or male principle, is logic, action, discipline, dryness, and the mind. Combined, they produce life. Out of balance, they bring misery, as the story of the Moon Lady and Master Archer suggests.

Ying-ying's name, which means "clear reflection," represents an amalgam of the two concepts. She illustrates problems occurring when life is not in balance. Her fascination with her shadow represents her yin, her undisciplined emotions. Her fall into the lake immerses her in yin and separates her from the yang, the structure and order, of her family. She is too young to handle so much chaos. Her response, suggested in the opening paragraphs, is to go too far the other way, hiding her yin and living entirely in yang. The reader will see the consequences of such an approach in future stories.

The second motif is specific to this story alone: the shadow. Ying-ying mentions it in the second paragraph, saying that she kept her real personality hidden "like a small shadow." As a child she is amazed by it, saying, "I loved my shadow, this dark side of me that had my same restless nature." The shadow represents Ying-ying's emotions—her active, spirited self—her yin.

After nearly drowning, fearing for her life among strangers and being unable to locate her family among the throngs on the lake, Ying-ying states, "I felt I was lost forever." The next mention of her shadow parallels that emotional state. Her rescuers leave her on the dock, and she sees her shadow again, "shorter this time, shrunken and wild-looking."

The play Ying-ying watches from the bushes is done in silhouette, shadows against a screen. In it she sees a statement of Chinese belief about the true nature of women and men. Taking action has caused Ying-ying to ruin her clothes and to fall off the boat. Taking action also causes the Moon Lady's woes. Ying-ying says of the Moon Lady, "I understood her grief. In one small moment, we had both lost the world, and there was no way to get it back."

Ying-ying is too young to understand that the Moon Lady is an actor. When the young man offers the granting of a wish for a donation, Ying-ying says, "nobody was listening to him, except my shadow and me in the bushes." Thinking it is really Chang-o, she runs up "to the other side of the moon" with her wish. What looked in shadow like a beautiful woman turns out to be a man with "shrunken cheeks, a broad oily nose, large glaring teeth, ... red-stained eyes ... [and] a [tired] face." This Chang-o will not grant her wish.

Her family is gone, Amah is gone, and she can't even trust her own perceptions. Ying-ying's world is as lost to her as the Moon Lady's. She recalls that both her wish and being found by her family "seemed an illusion ... a wish granted that could not be trusted." The reader will see in the other stories that Ying-ying spends the rest of her life trying to understand what she can trust, not only in the external world, but also in herself.

The reader must reflect on Ying-ying's statement, "I never believed my family found the same girl" in order to understand her opening remarks describing both herself and her daughter as "unseen and not seeing, unheard and not hearing, unknown by others." Even more pain lies in her future stories, ultimately leading her to keep her "true nature" safely hidden. This decision offers a measure of safety, but it also robs her of her energetic, trusting spirit. She remains tragically "out of balance" most of her life.

Study Questions

1. Who is Amah? Baba?

2. What plans has the family made to celebrate the Moon Festival?

3. What does Ying-ying describe as "this dark side of me that had my same restless nature"?

4. Why does Amah say Ying-ying's mother will banish them both to Kunming?

5. What does Ying-ying mistake for a swimming snake, one of the Five Evils?

6. How do her rescuers know that Ying-ying is from a wealthy family?

7. According to Chinese tradition, why does the Moon Lady live apart from her husband?

8. Where is Ying-ying as she watches the play?

9. Ying-ying is unable to remember what her wish was until when?

10. What was her wish?

Answers

1. Amah is Ying-ying's nanny. Baba is Ying-ying's father.

2. The family has rented a large boat on Tai Lake and has made arrangements for special foods. A ceremony will take place during the evening.

3. She describes her shadow this way.

4. Ying-ying had ruined her special new clothes by smearing blood all over them.

5. Ying-ying thinks the fishing net that rescues her is one of the Five Evils.

6. The woman notices Ying-ying's pale skin and soft feet, like one who had led a pampered, indoor life.

7. Chang-o, the Moon Lady, lives in the moon as a consequence of stealing and eating the peach of immortality, which was intended for her husband, the Master Archer.

8. She is hiding in the bushes on shore, near the stage.

9. Ying-ying remembers her wish when she is an old woman, on the day of the Moon Festival, as she tells this story.

10. She wanted her family to find her.

Suggested Essay Topics

1. At the beginning of this story, Ying-ying describes herself as "lost." In what ways is that statement foreshadowed in "The Joy Luck Club"?

2. Explain the symbolism of Ying-ying's shadow.

3. Describe the expectations of women in China as they are revealed in this story. Consider expectations of Ying-ying, her mother, and Amah. Compare and contrast them with the expectations for Lindo in "The Red Candle."

The Twenty-Six Malignant Gates

Vignette

Summary

A mother tells her seven-year-old daughter not to ride her bicycle around the corner. When the daughter wants to know why, the mother says the daughter will fall and the mother will not see or hear her. When the daughter asks how her mother knows this will happen, her mother replies that it is written in *The Twenty-Six Malignant Gates*, as are all the bad things that can happen to children who are away from their mothers. The daughter wants to see the book, but the mother says it is written in Chinese and she will not understand it. The daughter asks what the 26 bad things are in the book, but her mother does not answer; she sits and knits. The daughter repeats the question, and still her mother does not answer. The daughter decides her mother doesn't know what they are and, further, doesn't know anything at all. She jumps on her bike, pedals furiously toward the corner, and falls before she gets there.

Analysis

This vignette, like the first one, consists of archetypal characters. Readers should resist the temptation to identify the mother of this piece as Suyuan or Lindo, the daughter as Jing-mei or Waverly.

The young woman who brought the swan and all her good intentions to America now has the daughter she dreamed of. Her Chinese approach to motherhood insists upon obedience; however, this trait does not come easily to her American-born daughter. The mother wants to protect her daughter from harm, but the daughter takes risks finding things out for herself. The mother is quiet and calm, a typical Chinese woman; her daughter is loud and active, a typical American child. The mother wants her daughter to trust her; she says, "You must listen to me." The daughter, though, wants to make up her own mind; she tells her mother, "You don't know anything!" In her rebellion she discovers just the opposite.

All four stories in this section share this underlying conflict of the daughters' desire for independence in conflict with the mothers' guidance. We might call it, to paraphrase the title of an early 1960s sitcom, "Mother Knows Best."

Study Questions

1. How old is the daughter?
2. What does the mother tell the daughter not to do?
3. Why does the mother tell her this?
4. What is *The Twenty-Six Malignant Gates*?
5. Why does the daughter want to see the book?
6. Why won't the mother show her daughter the book?
7. When the mother refuses, what does the daughter demand?
8. How does the mother respond to the demand?
9. What does the daughter accuse her mother of?
10. Where is the daughter when she falls off her bicycle?

Answers

1. The daughter is seven.
2. She tells her not to ride her bicycle around the corner.
3. She wants to be close by if her daughter gets hurt.

4. *The Twenty-Six Malignant Gates* is a Chinese book that lists dangers children can get into.

5. She doesn't believe her mother.

6. The mother says the book is written in Chinese and the daughter would not understand it.

7. The daughter wants to know what the 26 bad things are.

8. She says nothing.

9. The daughter says her mother doesn't know what the 26 things are and that she doesn't know anything at all.

10. She is not even at the corner.

Suggested Essay Topics

1. Discuss this vignette as a clash of cultures, typical of immigrant families.

2. Discuss this vignette as a clash of generations, typical of all families.

Rules of the Game

New Characters:

Waverly Jong: *Lindo's only daughter and youngest child; narrator*

Vincent and Winston Jong: *Lindo's older brothers*

Lau Po: *an old man in the park who helps Waverly learn chess*

Summary

The adult Waverly looking back on her childhood tells this story. An incident with her mother and some salted plums teaches her "the art of invisible strength," encapsuled in two sayings: "Bite back your tongue" and "Strongest wind cannot be seen."

One year at a Christmas celebration at the First Chinese Baptist Church, Vincent gets a used chess set; Waverly selects a box of Life Savers; and Winston receives a kit for a model submarine. Once home, Waverly offers two of her Life Savers to substitute for the missing two chessmen if Vincent will let her play. The winner could eat both Life Savers.

When Waverly starts asking too many questions, Vincent hands her the manual and tells her to read the rules for herself. Her mother encourages this, saying that immigrants are often not told all the rules so that they don't get ahead of the local people. Waverly begins to study chess seriously.

In addition to learning each piece and the different moves, she comes to understand the importance of strategy and the value of not revealing her plans. She becomes so involved in chess that she makes a chessboard, hangs it on the wall in her bedroom, and stares at it for hours, playing imaginary games. Soon her brothers no longer play with her.

Waverly begins playing chess in the playground at the end of the alley with an old man named Lau Po. At first she loses, but Lau Po teaches her both strategies and chess etiquette. On weekends small crowds gather as Waverly defeats opponent after opponent. Even Lindo comes to watch, sitting proudly on the bench while humbly declaring, "Is luck."

Someone suggests that Waverly compete in area chess tournaments. Waverly says, "I desperately wanted to go, but I bit back my tongue." Instead, she tells her mother she doesn't want to. "They would have American rules. If I lost, I would bring shame on my family." The technique works just as she wishes; Lindo insists that she try.

Waverly wins at that meet easily. As she continues to compete, Lindo encourages her all she can. The Chinese community also encourages her, and by the time she is nine, Waverly has become a national chess champion. On Saturday morning shopping expeditions, Lindo proudly tells everyone, "This my daughter Wavely Jong."

One Saturday Waverly expresses embarrassment at Lindo's pride. Her mother has nothing to say; the angry expression on her face says it all. Waverly runs away.

After a couple of hours, realizing she has nowhere else to go, she comes home. The family is having dinner, and Lindo has little to say. Waverly walks into her room, lies down, and tries to figure out what to do next.

Analysis

The title of this story, "Rules of the Game," works on three levels. Most obviously it refers to Waverly's learning the rules of chess. It also refers to Lindo's observation that immigrants must learn the rules of their adopted country for themselves, because the locals will not share them. Finally, it refers to Waverly's relationship with Lindo, which becomes a power struggle between the two. Learning the rules of chess takes up much of the plot of this story, but learning to get along with her mother will occupy the rest of the novel.

The theme of this story, "strongest wind cannot be seen" or "the greatest power lies in the unexpected," also works on multiple levels. In the opening paragraphs Waverly says this way of thinking helped her win arguments, respect, and chess games. "I discovered that for the whole game one must gather invisible strengths and see the endgame before the game begins." Waverly also learns to keep her strategy a secret. "A little knowledge withheld is a great advantage one should store for future use." At her first chess tournament Waverly keeps her secrets so well that her opponent never sees defeat coming.

Waverly's failure to "bite back [her] tongue," issuing her challenge to Lindo even though she "knew it was a mistake to say anything more," has disastrous consequences. Lindo cannot tolerate such disrespect as a mother and especially as a Chinese mother dealing with a daughter. She switches from "protective ally" to opponent. Waverly is about to learn that her mother does indeed know how to play chess, how to be the "strongest wind."

Tan underscores the analogy of Waverly and Lindo's relationship to a chess game subtly. Vincent explains that there are 16 chess pieces per player. When Waverly returns home after running away, she says, "I climbed the 16 steps to the door. . .." The apartment thus becomes a metaphoric chess board on which Waverly and Lindo play out their game.

When Waverly runs away, she envisions Lindo walking through the streets looking for her, then going home to wait. She does not foresee that Lindo gathers invisible strengths. She is calmly eating supper with the family when Waverly appears at the door. Like a good chess player, Lindo does not reveal her strategy. She bites back her tongue and says only, "We not concerning this girl. This girl not have concerning for us." No scolding, no punishment: Waverly has no idea what will happen next. The reader, however, may well suspect that she will have a hard time outmanipulating this opponent. From "The Red Candle" we already know that Lindo knows how to use secrets to her advantage.

Like the woman with the swan feather in the first vignette, Lindo wants a better life for her daughter. Waverly grows up in a warm, loving home in a supportive community. She does not appreciate what she has, though: She thinks her success is due entirely to her own efforts. While she certainly has dedicated a great deal of time and effort to the game, she has not been alone in her pursuit. She owes a debt to her brothers, who sleep in the living room and do her chores so she can study chess; to Lau Po, who has taught her his secrets; and to her mother, who has shown her love, pride, and support in many ways. Unfortunately, Waverly does not recognize this. Her comment, "If you want to show off, then why don't you learn to play chess?" reveals self-centeredness, an attitude Lindo had not envisioned in her daughter. In the power struggle between the two, Lindo has the next move.

Study Questions

1. When Waverly wants the salted plums, what does her mother tell her?

2. What was the inspiration for Waverly's name?

3. How does Lindo react when Waverly asks her what Chinese torture is?

4. What gift does Waverly receive for Christmas?

5. Where does Waverly meet Lau Po?

6. How does Waverly manipulate her mother into letting her compete in a local chess tournament?

7. In what ways does Lindo encourage Waverly?

8. To whom does Lindo brag about Waverly's success?

9. When Waverly says she wishes Lindo wouldn't tell everyone she is her daughter, what does Lindo think she means?

10. How does Lindo "bite back her tongue" in the closing scene?

Answers

1. Lindo says, "Bite back your tongue" in the store. Later she adds, "Strongest wind cannot be seen."

2. Waverly was named after the street on which the family lives; but her family calls her "Meimei" or "Little Sister," because she is the youngest and the only girl.

3. She asks where Waverly has heard the expression. When Waverly says "some boy" at school said it, Lindo calmly replies that Chinese people are involved in all kinds of professions; they are not lazy like Americans. She also says Chinese people do the best torture there is.

4. Waverly receives a box of Life Savers.

5. She meets him in the playground at the end of the alley.

6. Waverly pretends she does not want to compete because she will lose. Lindo then insists that she try.

7. Lindo gives Waverly her *chang*, displays her trophies, offers advice on playing chess, lets her compete in tournaments farther and farther from home, makes her two new dresses, makes her brothers do her chores, makes her brothers sleep in the living room, does not insist that she clean her plate, and brags about her.

8. Lindo tells everyone she sees about Waverly's success.

9. Lindo thinks Waverly is ashamed or embarrassed to be her daughter.

10. When Waverly returns from running away, Lindo does not lecture or scold her. She ignores her, saying that if Waverly doesn't care about her family, her family will not care about her.

Suggested Essay Topics

1. What does Waverly learn about playing chess? (Consider breaking this question into three parts: individual moves, etiquette, and overall strategy.)

2. In what ways does the story compare the relationship between Waverly and Lindo to a chess game?

3. The adult Waverly, looking back, says of her mother, "I think she thought of herself as my protective ally." Is this an accurate assessment of Lindo's attitude toward Waverly's talent and success? Explain.

The Voice from the Wall

New Characters:

Lena St. Clair: *Ying-ying's daughter, 10 years old at the time of this story*

Clifford St. Clair: *Ying-ying's husband, Lena's father*

Teresa Sorci and Mrs. Sorci: *neighbors in the St. Clairs' apartment building. Teresa is about 12 years old. Her bedroom is next to Lena's*

Summary

The adult Lena narrates this story. As a child she wondered about "the death of a thousand cuts," in which a condemned man is sliced away little by little until he dies. Her great-grandfather had once ordered someone to die in this manner, and the ghost of the executed man returned and killed him. "Either that," she says, "or he died of influenza a week later."

Lena imagines her great-grandfather's last moments. The ghost appears, saying he thought the worst that could happen to him was this torturous execution. "But I was wrong," he says. "The worst is on the other side," meaning the other side of life—death. In her daydream the ghost then drags her great-grandfather from this world through the wall to the other side.

When Lena was five, she fell down the basement stairs. Ying-ying told her to stay out of the basement because an evil man who had lived there thousands of years would impregnate her and eat her family. After that Lena saw danger everywhere with her "Chinese eyes," she says, "the part of me I got from my mother."

Communication in the family is poor. Ying-ying warns Lena about dangers all around her, but Lena knows Ying-ying makes things up when challenged. Ying-ying's English is poor and St. Clair's Chinese worse, so communication between the parents is tenuous. Sometimes her father makes up what he thinks Ying-ying says. Lena also makes things up to her advantage when translating for either parent.

When Lena is 10, the family moves to North Beach, an Italian neighborhood of San Francisco. Lena adjusts easily to the noise and smells, but Ying-ying has trouble. The house is on a hill so steep that Ying-ying says a person's life is always rolling backward. She tries to restore balance by rearranging the furniture several times. Her father dismissively claims, "Your mother is just practicing her nesting instincts." A few days later, a new baby crib in Lena's room suggests he may be right. Lena notices other, ominous signs, though, and she worries.

Lena hears her neighbors, the Sorcis, shouting at night. Then she hears what sounds like someone being killed with the death of a thousand cuts. The next night she hears it again. She meets the girl she believes to be the victim one day and is surprised that she looks so happy. Lena feels guilty for knowing the truth about her.

One day Suyuan and Canning Woo pick up Lena at school and take her to the hospital to visit her mother. Ying-ying's baby was born with a severe birth defect and is dead. Ying-ying is incoherent, and St. Clair asks Lena to translate; but her words seem like insanity to Lena, so she makes up a translation.

Ying-ying enters a deep depression, unable to function. St. Clair tries to convince Lena and himself she is just tired, but Lena is frightened. When she hears the Sorcis fighting at night, she is comforted by thinking that someone else's life is worse than hers.

One evening, however, the doorbell rings and the girl next door, Teresa, walks through the apartment to Lena's bedroom and climbs out the window. Her mother has kicked her out in one of their arguments. Teresa wants to climb back into her bedroom via the

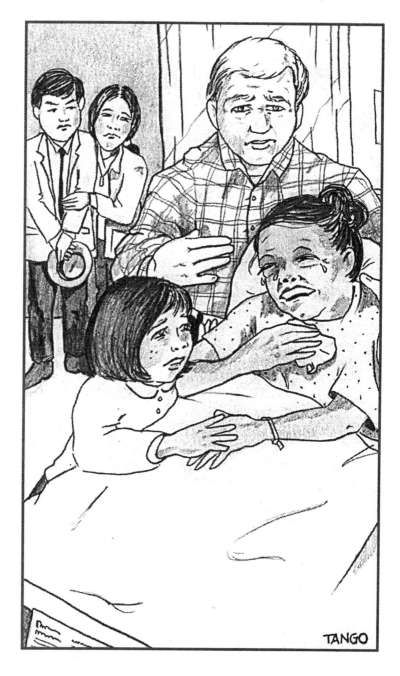

fire escape. When Lena asks if Mrs. Sorci will be angry, Teresa casually says that they fight like this "all the time."

Later that night Lena hears Teresa and her mother shouting at each other, but this time she also hears the love between them. She lies in her bed and cries, happy to have misjudged them.

That experience brings Lena hope. Her mother is still depressed, but Lena believes it will pass. She envisions a mother being sentenced to the death of a thousand cuts and being told, "It is the only way to save you." The sword goes up and down, but no harm is done. The mother understands that she has already been through the worst possible. Then the daughter reaches out and pulls her mother back through the wall.

Analysis

The title "The Voice from the Wall" refers to three parts or voices. The first is the ghost returning from "the other side" for Lena's great-grandfather. His voice threatens doom. The second voices belong to Teresa Sorci and her mother. They demonstrate love. Finally, Lena herself near the end of the story tries to bring her mother back from the other side of her depression. Hers is a voice of hope. The arguments between Teresa and her mother form an important part of the plot; both the image of the ghost and Lena's struggle, while more subtle, underscore a theme of dealing with adversity.

When Tan sets the St. Clair family next to the Sorcis, she emphasizes their differences. The St. Clairs, Chinese-Americans, are quiet; the Sorcis, Italian-Americans, are loud. The St. Clairs are gentle with each other; the Sorcis are violent. The St. Clairs communicate almost by guessing; the Sorcis make their thoughts known not only to each other but also to the neighbors. The St. Clairs live in fantasy worlds: Clifford, by making up what he wants his wife to have said; Ying-ying, by retreating into her pain; Lena, by thinking she knows everything about Teresa Sorci. The Sorcis, on the other hand, live without illusions. Teresa tells Lena exactly what her mother is thinking, what she will do, and how she will react. She is also confident of her mother's love. Strengths and weaknesses exist in both apartments.

The story of the ghost and Lena's great-grandfather parallels the circumstances surrounding Lena and Ying-ying. Lena envisions the ghost "looking like a smashed vase hastily put back together" when he returns to exact his revenge. She compares her mother's depression to that kind of death, saying Ying-ying's fears "devoured her, piece by piece." Lena's world is as shattered as both the ghost and her mother. She describes Ying-ying's despondency as "the worst possible thing," in part because the stability of her family has been destroyed. While communication has never been a strength in the St. Clair household, Lena usually knew what to expect. Now her mother's sorrow is a wall she can only dream of penetrating.

This story is one of the best in the novel at transcending the specific circumstances of Chinese women who raise American children. Sometimes funny, sometimes tragic, always complex, the St. Clair family represents every family at one time or another. Clifford St. Clair exemplifies not just an American who speaks minimal Chinese but also every husband who doesn't try very hard to understand his wife. Ying-ying, in addition to being an immigrant who speaks English poorly, represents every wife who pleases her husband when he's around and does what she wants when he's gone. What child hasn't taken advantage of a parent's ignorance at one time or another? Lena manipulates the language weaknesses of both her parents to her advantage, one time to gain a metal lunch box, much later to escape a situation beyond her comprehension. The cultural aspects of the characters become secondary in these contexts.

Study Questions

1. What is the death of a thousand cuts?
2. Why does Lena see danger everywhere?
3. Why doesn't Lena look Chinese?
4. Who changes Ying-ying's name to Betty?
5. Why is communication so difficult at the St. Clair household?
6. Where is the family's new apartment?
7. Why does Ying-ying's baby die?
8. How does Ying-ying react to the loss of her baby?
9. Why does Teresa come to the St. Clairs' apartment?
10. Near the end of the story, why does Lena cry when she hears Teresa and her mother yelling at each other at night?

Answers

1. In the death of a thousand cuts, a man's body is sliced away little by little until he dies.

2. Lena sees danger everywhere after she falls down the basement stairs, and Ying-ying makes up a story about an evil man who lives in the basement.

3. Lena's father is English-Irish.

4. Lena's father, Clifford St. Clair, changes her name to Betty.

5. Communication is difficult because Ying-ying speaks poor English, St. Clair speaks poor Chinese, and Lena understands what her mother says in Chinese but not what she means.

6. The family moves to an Italian neighborhood in San Francisco, North Beach.

7. The baby dies because of a severe birth defect.

8. Ying-ying becomes unable to function; she is very depressed.

9. Teresa wants to climb out Lena's bedroom window onto the fire escape, so she can climb in her own bedroom window.

10. Lena is happy to be wrong about Teresa.

Suggested Essay Topics

1. Lena refers to her "Chinese eyes." Explain what she means on a literal and figurative level.

2. In what ways do problems in communication affect the St. Clair family?

Half and Half

New Characters:

Rose Hsu Jordan: *narrator of this story, daughter of An-mei and George, wife of Ted Jordan; a free-lance production assistant for graphic artists*

Ted Jordan: *Rose's husband, a dermatologist*

Mrs. Jordan: *Ted's mother*

George Hsu: *An-mei's father*

Janice, Ruth, Matthew, Mark, Luke, and Bing Hsu: *Rose's sisters and brothers*

Summary

Rose, the narrator, describes a "white leatherette Bible" her mother uses to prop up one leg of a crooked table. After spending more than 20 years on the floor, it is still "clean white." As she looks at it, Rose wonders how she will tell An-mei that she and Ted are getting a divorce. She knows her mother will insist that she try to save her marriage.

At the beginning of Rose and Ted's relationship, both mothers object to their dating because of the difference in race. Their parents' opposition draws them closer together, and they are married just before Ted begins medical school.

Rose and Ted have an unusual relationship: He makes all the decisions because she wants him to. Ted becomes dissatisfied with this arrangement after losing a malpractice suit. He begins to insist that Rose choose. Finally, he tells her he wants a divorce. Rose is devastated.

Rose reflects on her mother's faith, which An-mei mispronounces as "fate." Rose wonders whether hope might be all that people can really have, and says the day she started wondering about this was the same day An-mei lost her faith in God.

The story flashes back to the day when Rose, 14, and her family go to the beach. When her father decides to go fishing and her sisters race down the beach, Rose watches her four brothers. The three older boys play together, but Bing, age 4, wanders down the beach. Rose warns him to stay away from the water.

Later Bing walks out on the reef where his father is fishing. As Rose watches, he falls into the water and is never seen again.

The next morning An-mei, who has never driven before, takes Rose back to the reef along with the white Bible, a thermos, and a teacup. An-mei holds the Bible and prays aloud in Chinese for the return of Bing, alive. At the end of her prayer, she waits. Three times she thinks she sees him, but each time "Bing" becomes a mass of seaweed.

An-mei puts the Bible down and takes the thermos and teacup to the edge of the water. She pours sweetened tea from the thermos into the teacup and throws it into the sea, and she adds a blue sapphire ring. For the next hour all they see is seaweed; then An-mei glances down the beach and sees Bing walking toward them. Rose does, too. Or they think they do. He lights a cigarette, and they realize he is a stranger.

Rose wants to leave, but An-mei is undaunted. She believes Bing is in a cave in the reef. She pulls a large inner tube out of the trunk of the car, ties the line from her husband's fishing pole around it and throws it into the sea, holding on to the pole. She tells Rose that the inner tube will go where Bing is and help him out of the cave and back to them. Eventually the line snaps, and An-mei and Rose scramble to watch it travel across the cove. A wave forces it first against the wall and then into a cavern under the surface. The tube floats in and out several times until finally it comes out "torn and lifeless." When that happens, An-mei abandons the search.

The story returns to the present. Rose never expected to find Bing that day, and she does not expect to save her marriage. Her mother insists that she must try and leaves Rose alone to think about why. Rose says she had known Bing was in danger and did nothing; she also knew her marriage was in danger and did nothing. In a moment of insight, she realizes that faith balances the loss caused by fate. She thinks that An-mei still pays attention to the loss of Bing. To confirm her suspicions, she takes the Bible out from under the table leg and opens it to find what An-mei wrote in it before she used it to prop up the table leg: Bing's name appears in pencil on the page marked "Deaths."

Analysis

This story returns to the motif of yin and yang, beginning with the title, a reference to the Daoist ideal of two halves balancing to make a whole. Rose and Ted's relationship is an example of yin and yang gone awry. Instead of balancing the characteristics of both yin and yang in her personality, Rose is entirely yin, always the victim. Ted, on the other hand, is all yang, always the rescuer. Unhealthy though their relationship is, it works until Ted loses the malpractice suit and becomes the one in need. Rose, unaware of how hard he has taken the loss, does not help him. The balance destroyed, their marriage falls apart.

Balance is the key to the theme of this story, suggesting our lives are shaped both by what we control and what we don't control. Echoing the theme of "The Joy Luck Club," it suggests that hope is all people really have. Rose says of her own hope, "I was not denying any possibility, good or bad. I was just saying, If there is a choice, dear God or whatever you are, here's where the odds should be placed."

When An-mei returns with Rose to the site of Bing's drowning, she has complete confidence one of her three plans will work. First she uses her Christian faith, holding the white Bible and praying to God. When Bing does not appear, she turns to her Chinese tradition. Explaining that an ancestor had once stolen sacred water, she throws tea into the sea to "sweeten the temper of the Coiling Dragon." She also throws in a blue sapphire ring, possibly her most valuable possession, a gift from her mother. When he still does not reappear, An-mei falls back on her *nengkan,* the powerful self-confidence that has served her family so well in the past. She is convinced her own efforts will succeed where Christian faith and Chinese tradition have failed: the inner tube attached to her husband's fishing pole will go where Bing is and bring him back. But when the fishing line snaps, she no longer has the "illusion that somehow [she's] in control." She and Rose can only watch powerlessly and hopefully as the inner tube is smashed against the cove wall until it is destroyed.

"At that moment, and not until that moment, did she give up," Rose says, adding, "It made me angry—so blindingly angry—that everything had failed us."

The story concludes that fate consists of expectation—a positive force, yang—coupled with inattention—a negative force, yin. Those who lose something they love, as An-mei lost Bing and Rose lost Ted, must fill the void, must "pay attention to what [was] lost." The family Bible's clean condition tells the reader that An-mei notices it even though she pretends not to. It represents the absent Bing. Bing's name written "in erasable pencil" in it suggests that An-mei, like Rose, now believes hope is the most a person can have. Rose must pay attention to her marriage, something she acknowledges she has not done, in order to restore the balance in her life. This is her fate.

Study Questions

1. How does Rose describe her mother's skill as housekeeper?

2. What word does An-mei use to describe Ted when she meets him?

3. What nationality does Mrs. Jordan believe Rose is?

4. Describe Rose and Ted's relationship.

5. What event causes a change in their relationship?

6. What is *nengkan?*

7. Why doesn't Bing play with Matthew, Mark, and Luke at the beach?

8. What symbols does An-mei use to try to bring Bing back?

9. How does An-mei react when Rose announces her divorce?

10. What evidence suggests that An-mei never completely abandons hope that Bing will return?

Answers

1. Rose says, "My mother is not the best housekeeper in the world."

2. An-mei calls Ted a *waigoren,* a foreigner.

3. She thinks Rose is Vietnamese.

4. Rose is all yin and Ted is all yang. Before they are married, she is always "the damsel in distress," and he is "the knight in shining armor." After the marriage the pattern continues, with Rose always passive and Ted always making decisions.

5. When Ted loses the malpractice lawsuit, he is the weak one in need of Rose's support. Rose does not realize this because it has never happened before. He begins to insist she make decisions.

6. *Nengkan* is the ability to do whatever you put your mind to, absolute self-confidence.

7. The older boys think Bing will ruin their sand castle because he is so much younger.

8. An-mei uses the white leatherette Bible, sweetened tea and a sapphire ring, and an inner tube.

9. An-mei tells Rose to try to save her marriage.

10. First, Bing's name is written in the Bible so it will be easy to erase. Second, the Bible is very clean, even though it has been on the floor more than 20 years, and An-mei is not the best of housekeepers.

Suggested Essay Topics

1. Explain how the motif of yin and yang figures in this story.

2. This story touches on the issue of racial discrimination. In what ways is the author's depiction of both An-mei's and Mrs. Jordan's attitude accurate?

Two Kinds

New Character:

Old Chong: *Jing-mei's deaf piano teacher*

Summary

This story is narrated by the adult Jing-mei looking back on her childhood piano lessons.

When Jing-mei is nine, Suyuan wants her to be a prodigy like Lindo's daughter and Shirley Temple. Jing-mei at first agrees, but after repeatedly failing to find her special talent, she quits trying.

A few months later Suyuan notices a young Chinese girl playing piano on "The Ed Sullivan Show". Three days afterward she announces that she has made arrangements for Jing-mei to take piano lessons from Mr. Chong. Jing-mei quickly discovers he can't tell when she is making mistakes because he is deaf. As long as she maintains the right tempo, "Old Chong" thinks she is doing well.

The adult Jing-mei interrupts here to observe, "Maybe I never really gave myself a chance. I did pick up the basics pretty quickly, and I might have become a good pianist at that young age. But I was…determined not to try."

After about a year of half-hearted effort, Jing-mei enters a talent competition. Instead of memorizing the music in preparation, however, she practices her fancy curtsy. The night of the recital, in front of an audience that includes all the Joy Luck Club aunties and uncles, Jing-mei plays very badly. She gets the fancy curtsy right, but the audience is silent, except for Old Chong, who shouts, "Bravo! Bravo! Well done!" Jing-mei sees Suyuan's "stricken face" in the audience and tries not to cry as she sits down, ashamed.

She thinks her piano lessons are behind her, but the next afternoon, Suyuan reminds her it's time to practice. When she refuses, they argue. Jing-mei shouts that she wishes she weren't Suyuan's daughter. She wishes she were dead, like Suyuan's two daughters in China. Suyuan, stunned, leaves the room. The piano lessons are over.

The adult Jing-mei comments that she disappointed her mother again and again in later years when she insisted on the right to be less than her best. She finds her old recital piece in the piano

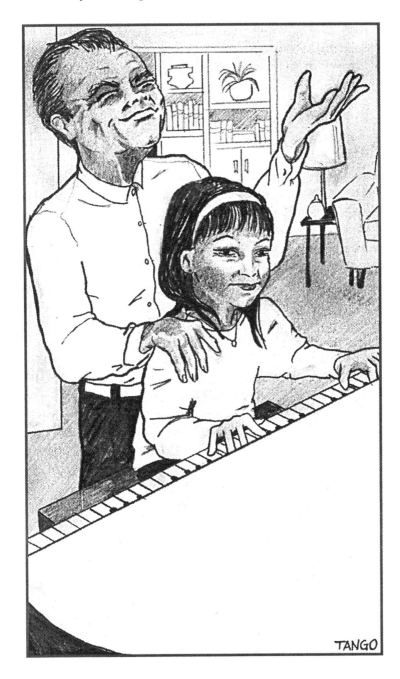

bench and begins to play it. Then she notices the piece on the page opposite, "Perfectly Contented." After she plays through both pieces, she realizes they are "two halves of the same song."

Analysis

Hope was the basis for founding the original Joy Luck Club in Kweilin. At the end of "The Joy Luck Club," Jing-mei observes that the aunties "see daughters who will bear grandchildren born without any connecting hope passed from generation to generation." Hope is both theme and motif in this story. The opening paragraphs remind the reader of how much Suyuan lost in China, emphasizing her dreams for a new life in America. These ambitions extend to Jing-mei as well, connecting mother and daughter.

Suyuan's declaration to Jing-mei, "You can be best anything," reveals her appreciation of the opportunities available in America. Jing-mei shares her mother's enthusiasm at first, believing that her prodigy side, symbolized by her Peter Pan haircut, will be perfect. As she fails test after test, however, she says, "I hated . . . the raised hopes and failed expectations." Frustrated, she quits trying, and eventually so does her mother. Jing-mei says, "At last she was beginning to give up hope." The young Chinese piano player on "The Ed Sullivan Show", however, changed that.

The argument about continuing piano lessons lasts until Jing-mei mentions Suyuan's lost twins. The reader will recall from "The Joy Luck Club" that Suyuan never stopped hoping to see her daughters again. Jing-mei's childish anger creates an image greater than Suyuan can bear: "her face went blank, her mouth closed, her arms went slack, and she backed out of the room, stunned, as if she were blowing away like a small brown leaf, thin, brittle, lifeless." Ironically, Jing-mei wonders later why her mother had given up hope, as the piano sits in the living room, its lid shut against "dust, my misery, and her dreams." She never connects the hopes for one daughter with the hope of seeing the other two.

Jing-mei's observation that "Pleading Child" and "Perfectly Contented" are "two halves of the same song" returns the reader to the motif of yin and yang that runs throughout the novel. "Pleading Child" was the "simple, moody" piece from the recital, which now looks "more difficult than I remembered." "Perfectly Contented" is lighter, longer, faster, and just as easy. The titles suggest Jing-mei's attitude as a child and as an adult. Not until later in the novel will she realize where her refusal to strive for the best has led her.

Study Questions

1. Suyuan wants Jing-mei to be a prodigy, just like what two people?

2. Where does Suyuan get ideas to test for Jing-mei's ability?

3. Why can't "Old Chong" tell when Jing-mei is playing badly?

4. Why does Jing-mei rebel against her mother's hopes for her musical ability?

5. Who says, "You aren't a genius like me"?

6. To what two kinds of daughters does Suyuan refer?

7. How does Jing-mei end the argument about her piano lessons?

8. What other disappointments does Jing-mei mention that she caused Suyuan?

9. When does Suyuan give Jing-mei the piano?

10. In what way does Jing-mei describe "Pleading Child" and "Perfectly Contented"?

Answers

1. The two model prodigies are Lindo's daughter, Waverly, and Shirley Temple.

2. Suyuan reads articles about gifted children in the magazines of the houses she cleans.

3. "Old Chong" is deaf, and Jing-mei deliberately deceives him.

4. Jing-mei overhears Suyuan bragging to Lindo about Jing-mei's talent.

5. Waverly says this to Jing-mei after the talent show.

6. She refers to obedient and disobedient daughters.

7. She says she wishes she were dead like Suyuan's twin daughters in China.

8. She didn't get straight A's, didn't become class president, didn't get into Stanford, and didn't finish college. Each time she insisted she had the right to be less than her best.

9. The piano is a gift for her thirtieth birthday.

10. They are two halves of the same song.

Suggested Essay Topics

1. In what ways does Jing-mei misunderstand Suyuan's hopes in this story?

2. In what ways do "Pleading Child" and "Perfectly Contented" describe Jing-mei?

American Translation

Vignette

Summary

The mother insists her adult daughter move the mirrored armoire at the foot of her bed. She says her daughter's "marriage happiness" will reflect off the mirror and turn to unhappiness. The daughter, annoyed, says there is no other place in the bedroom of the new condominium to put it. It will have to stay where it is.

The mother pulls a mirror, her housewarming present, out of a used Macy's shopping bag. She tells her daughter to mount this mirror above the head of the bed, across from the other mirror, so the reflections will "multiply your peach-blossom luck."

When the daughter asks what peach-blossom luck is, the mother only smiles mischievously, tells her to look in the mirror, and asks, "Am I not right? In this mirror is my future grandchild, already sitting on my lap next spring." The daughter looks and— yes, there it is!—her reflection.

Analysis

The mother in this vignette invokes the Chinese tradition of *feng shui*, which holds that locations can be lucky or unlucky. *Feng shui* influences Chinese and Chinese American architectural styles, building locations, and even furniture arrangement. Telling her daughter to move the mirror is one more way this mother tries to ensure her daughter's happiness.

The daughter does not understand the theories of *feng shui* or her mother's purpose in predicting trouble, nor does she care. She knows what she wants; the armoire will stay where it is. The mother compromises with the second mirror and defines "peach-blossom luck," children, as a desirable trait in a marriage.

Both "The Joy Luck Club" and "Two Kinds" point to a hope connecting generations. One of the characteristics of contemporary American society has been couples who delay starting a family or who decide not to have children at all. The daughter in this vignette has no children yet, and her mother encourages her to start a family. Otherwise, there may be no generation to pass hope on to.

This vignette introduces four stories told by the daughters, now adults in their thirties. Like the daughter who looks into the mirror, the daughters in these stories see and do not see what their mothers try to show them.

Study Questions

1. What is a "mirrored armoire"?

2. Where is the armoire?

3. According to the mother, why shouldn't the mirror be at the foot of the bed?

4. Why does the daughter refuse to move it?

5. Why is the daughter irritated?

6. How does the mother solve the problem?

7. What is the mother's housewarming present?

8. What is "peach-blossom luck"?

9. What does the mother see in the mirror?

10. What does the daughter see in the mirror?

Answers

1. An armoire is a cupboard or wardrobe (8 feet or taller) used before homes had built-in closets. This one has a mirror on it.

2. The armoire is at the foot of the bed in the bedroom of the daughter's new condominium.

3. The mother says the marriage happiness from the bed will bounce off the mirror and become its own opposite.

4. The armoire won't fit anywhere else.

5. The daughter has heard dire predictions all her life.

6. The mother says to place another mirror at the head of the bed.

7. Her housewarming gift is a gilt-edged mirror from the Price Club.

8. "Peach-blossom luck" means having children.

9. The mother sees her grandchild.

10. The daughter sees her own reflection.

Suggested Essay Topics

1. In what ways is the mother in this vignette living in the contemporary world, and in what ways is she living in the past?

2. In what ways do parents often try to transmit their values to their children?

Rice Husband

New Characters:

Harold Livotny: *Lena's husband, an architect*

Arnold Reisman: *a neighbor who was mean to Lena when they were children*

Summary

Ying-ying is visiting Lena, 36, and her husband, Harold, in their new home in Woodside. Lena worries that Ying-ying will see how precarious their marriage is.

The story flashes back to when Lena was eight. To encourage her to finish her food, Ying-ying told her that her future husband would have a pock mark on his face for every piece of rice she did not eat. Lena immediately thought of Arnold, a neighbor who had small marks about the size of grains of rice on his face and was mean to her. She was frightened she would have to marry him. At Sunday school later that week Lena saw a film about people with leprosy. She thought her mother would say their future spouses had left several meals unfinished. She tried to kill Arnold by not finishing her food, so she wouldn't have to marry him.

Five years later her father read in the paper one morning that Arnold had died of complications from a case of measles he'd had about the time Lena refused to finish her food. Lena felt responsible for his death, and that night she ate ice cream until she vomited.

The story returns to the present, with Lena observing that people get what they deserve. As evidence she cites her husband, Harold, whom she met eight years earlier at the architectural firm where both worked. They split the bill for working lunches in half, even though Lena's share was usually less than Harold's. Later they did the same when they met secretly for dinner. Lena didn't mind the unfairness.

Later she convinced Harold to start his own firm and offered to help finance it. He would not accept money from her under any business arrangement; instead, he invited her to move in with him and pay him $500 a month rent. Lena accepted, thrilled that they would be living together.

Both of them quit their jobs to work at this new business. Lena encouraged Harold not to give up and came up with some unusual ideas for restaurant designs. Harold used her ideas and became successful. The firm now employs 12 people, one of them Lena. Harold will not promote her, even though she is very good, saying the other employees will think the promotion is just because they are married. Lena feels that trying to keep things equal with Harold is not working any more.

The story returns to the present. Ying-ying looks at a tally of expenses on the refrigerator door, and Lena explains that they split expenses 50-50. Ying-ying notices Harold has put "ice cream" on his list and points out that Lena has never eaten it since Arnold died. She has always paid for half of it, though.

Lena shows Ying-ying to the guest room, a plain room decorated in Harold's taste. By the bed an unsteady table has a vase of freesias on it. Lena warns Ying-ying about it, then goes downstairs and marks

the ice cream off the refrigerator list. She and Harold argue about the way they split expenses until Lena hears the vase in the guest room fall and break. She goes upstairs and sees that the table has collapsed. Lena tells her mother she knew it would happen, and Ying-ying asks her why she didn't prevent it.

Analysis

Ying-ying's closing words to Lena, "Then why you don't stop it?" complete a motif that runs through this story, c*hunwang chihan*. The phrase literally means, "If the lips are gone, the teeth will be cold." Figuratively it suggests cause-and-effect relationships for everything that happens.

Referring to events in "The Voice from the Wall," Lena relates that Ying-ying knew her baby would be born dead, saying the family's home was built on a hill that was too steep. A Western reader might not see the *feng shui* cause and effect Ying-ying did, but would see clearly the relationship between Clifford St. Clair's bacon-and-egg breakfasts and his heart attack and death. The motif resurfaces when Ying-ying encourages Lena to eat by telling her leftover food will cause pock marks on her future husband's face. At first Lena eats, but later she decides against it. With the logic of an eight-year-old, she thinks this will kill Arnold, a mean neighbor she is afraid of having to marry. When the events surrounding Arnold's subsequent death appear to indicate she was right, she feels guilty and gorges herself on ice cream. The causes and effects exist only in the minds of the participants but are no less real for it.

Ying-ying criticizes Harold's table with "*Chunwang chihan*," wondering what to do with a table too unsteady for anything but a small vase of flowers. When the table falls, she points out that when the cause is obvious, the effect should be prevented.

This motif underscores the character development of both Harold and Lena. When Ying-ying tells Harold that Lena has "become so thin...you cannot see her," she is commenting on their marriage. She sees clearly what Lena denies: Harold abuses Lena's generosity and love when he insists that she pay for half of everything. "As long as we keep the money thing separate," he insists, "we'll always be sure of our love for each other." He uses their financial arrangement to ensure he has his way in every major decision. This pattern is so entrenched in their relationship that Lena does not even know how to articulate it at the end of the story.

Harold thinks Lena is talking about the cat when she brings up the subject of changing the way they manage household expenses. After all, she has gone along with everything up to now. At first it was just meals. Later he didn't want to accept her financial support for his firm on any businesslike basis such as a loan, which would benefit both equally. Instead, he exploited her by asking her to move in with him so he could start his business with her rent money. He now owns a very successful firm with 12 full-time employees, and Lena has nothing to show for her investment.

This pattern of Harold taking advantage of Lena continued into their marriage. It is present in their prenuptial agreement, in Harold's refusal to promote Lena even though she deserves it, in the uninviting style of their home, in their vacation plans, and in their day-to-day expenses. Lena has gone along with it, even though she recognizes that something is wrong. She values her contribution too little, afraid Harold might one day see her "as a sham of a woman." She considers herself lucky that Harold loves her but does not consider that Harold is lucky she loves him.

The wobbly table in the guest room symbolizes the couple. Lena wonders why Harold is proud of its clumsy design. The fragile legs will support their marble burden only as long as nothing jars the table. Similarly, Harold and Lena have a clumsy marriage, Lena often not saying what she is thinking, Harold pretty much getting whatever he wants. It is uneven and unfair, and something as small as a cat or a box of ice cream can shatter the assumptions that support it.

Study Questions

1. What omen told Ying-ying that her husband would die?

2. Where do Lena and Harold live?

3. What do Lena and Harold argue about just before Ying-ying comes to visit?

4. Why did Arnold die?

5. How did Lena and Harold meet?

6. Designing restaurants around a theme made Livotny & Associates very successful. Whose idea was this?

7. In her relationship with Harold, what is Lena afraid of?

8. Why does Harold insist they split expenses 50-50?

9. Why doesn't Lena eat ice cream?

10. What does the Chinese expression *chunwang chihan* mean?

Answers

1. A plant her husband had given her died even though she had watered it carefully.

2. They live in Woodside, in a renovated barn on four acres of land.

3. They argue about who should pay for exterminating the cat's fleas.

4. Arnold died of delayed complications from measles. Lena believed he died because she stopped eating her rice and other foods in hopes of not marrying him.

5. They both worked for Harned Kelley & Davis, an architectural firm.

6. Lena thought of this.

7. Lena is afraid Harold might leave her after seeing all her flaws.

8. Harold claims they will be sure of their love if they keep money out of the relationship.

9. After Arnold died, Lena felt guilty and ate ice cream until she vomited. She never ate it again.

10. *Chunwang chihan* means literally, "If the lips are gone, the teeth will be cold." Figuratively, it means "one thing is the result of another."

Suggested Essay Topics

1. Harold says, "As long as we keep the money thing separate, we'll always be sure of our love for each other." What evidence suggests that he is taking advantage of Lena by doing this?

2. What evidence suggests that Lena lacks self-esteem?

3. In what ways does Lena's submission to Harold's financial
    control parallel Ying-ying's submission to St. Clair's language
    control in "The Voice from the Wall"?

Four Directions

New Characters:

Mr. Rory: *Waverly's hairdresser*

Marlene Ferber: *Waverly's friend*

Marvin Chen: *Waverly's first husband*

Shoshana: *Waverly's and Marvin's daughter*

Rich Schields: *Waverly's fiancé, a tax attorney*

Lisa Lum: *Vincent Jong's girlfriend*

Summary

Waverly, age 36, describes meeting her mother for lunch in an
unsuccessful bid to tell her she's marrying Rich Schields. Lindo has
never met him, and she changes the subject whenever Waverly
mentions him. Waverly takes Lindo to her cluttered apartment to
show off a mink jacket, Rich's Christmas gift. Lindo criticizes its
poor quality and refuses to acknowledge the unmistakable signs
that Rich lives there.

Waverly comments that Lindo "knows how to hit a nerve." The
first time it happened, she was 10 and a chess champion. They
argued in the middle of a busy street and didn't speak to each other
for several days afterwards. Waverly said she wouldn't play chess
again. After another argument Waverly came down with chicken pox.

Lindo returned to her usual self during her daughter's illness.
Waverly returned to chess, but she noticed that Lindo didn't pay
as much attention to her success as she had before. She began to
lose more often. At 14, she quit.

Waverly thinks Lindo will criticize Rich a little at a time until it
ruins her feelings for him, as she did with Marvin, Shoshana's father.
Waverly doesn't want her mother to find flaws in Rich.

Finally, she figures out how to arrange for Rich to meet her parents. They visit Suyuan and Canning Woo one Sunday afternoon in time to be invited to stay for dinner. When she writes her thank-you note, she adds, "Rich said it was the best Chinese food he has ever tasted." Shortly afterward, Lindo invites Waverly to bring "a friend" for a birthday dinner for her father.

When they arrive, she notices Lindo's "forced smile" as she meets Rich. In the kitchen later Lindo remarks that Rich has "spots on his face" when asked what she thinks. At dinner Rich commits one error after another without even realizing it; at home he tells Waverly that he thinks everything went well.

The next day she drives back to her parents', determined both to announce her engagement and to confront Lindo. Her mother is sleeping on the sofa and looks dead. Waverly starts crying, causing Lindo to wake up, afraid something has happened. Waverly announces she's going to marry Rich and awaits Lindo's criticism.

To Waverly's surprise, her mother already knows they're getting married. Waverly stammers that she knows Lindo doesn't like Rich. Lindo is hurt Waverly thinks she would be so devious and accuses Waverly of being devious. Waverly, confused, says she isn't sure what's inside her. Half of her, Lindo explains, comes from her father's Cantonese family. The other half is from her mother's clan in Taiyuan. They have a pleasant conversation until Waverly confuses Taiyuan with Taiwan. To her they sound alike, but Lindo indignantly insists they are completely different.

Waverly doesn't understand the point, but she learns something about herself. She sees that the little girl who ran away from her mother years ago has been hiding. When she finally lets down her guard a little, she sees "an old woman, a wok for her armor, a knitting needle for her sword, getting a little crabby as she waited patiently for her daughter to invite her in."

The story shifts to the present. Waverly says she and Rich will postpone their wedding so they can honeymoon in China in October. Lindo mentions she plans to go back then, too, but not with them. Waverly knows Lindo really would like to travel with them. She knows it would be a disaster, but she also thinks it's a good idea.

Analysis

Tan returns to the motif of chess maneuvers to characterize the relationship between Waverly and Lindo. The story contains several allusions to chess, beginning with the argument on Stockton Street in "Rules of the Game". When Lindo does not speak to Waverly for a few days, Waverly recognizes a stratagem. Rather than responding in anger and falling into a trap, she, too, refuses to speak.

After a few days Waverly decides the next move is hers, and she stops playing chess. She even chooses "to sacrifice a tournament," as she might strategically give up a chess piece. When the tournament comes and goes and Lindo still does not speak, Waverly's next ploy is "to pretend to let her win" by announcing she wants to resume chess. She is startled when Lindo says "no." In a scene reminiscent of the ending of "Rules of the Game," she retreats to her bedroom and stares at her chessboard, trying to "undo this terrible mess."

Chicken pox returns the mother/daughter relationship to a semblance of normalcy. Waverly returns to competitive chess, but Lindo no longer offers her support. Waverly loses a tournament and reports that Lindo looked satisfied, "as if it had happened because she had devised this strategy."

As an adult, Waverly continues manipulating circumstances to her advantage. When Lindo refuses to react to the obvious signs that Rich lives with her, she devises a gambit to get her to meet him. It succeeds: after Waverly sends a thank-you note to Lindo's arch-rival Suyuan, telling her Rich said it was the best Chinese food he had ever eaten, Lindo invites Waverly to bring a friend over for dinner. Waverly knew Lindo would want to outdo Suyuan.

After the dinner, Waverly says, "In her hands I always became the pawn....And she was the queen." She visits her parents to announce her engagement and ends up talking with Lindo about her family background. At the end, she says, they have reached "a stalemate." Neither dominates the other.

Tan offers hope for reconciliation between the women when Waverly acknowledges that the problems in her relationship with Lindo are at least partly of her own making. Waverly also sees that

Lindo has not given up on her. The closing image, of Waverly, Rich, and Lindo flying to China together, "moving West to reach the East," evokes Jing-mei's observation in "The Joy Luck Club" that the East is "where things begin." In the next section "Double Face" reveals Lindo's attitude toward a new relationship with her daughter.

Study Questions

1. Why does Waverly invite Lindo to lunch?

2. How does Lindo respond to the evidence that Rich and Waverly live together?

3. After their argument, when does Lindo start treating Waverly normally again?

4. Why does Waverly worry about Lindo's criticism of Rich?

5. Who is Marvin Chen?

6. How does Waverly manipulate her mother into inviting Rich over for dinner?

7. What are three of Rich's gaffes during his visit with the Jongs?

8. When does Waverly tell Lindo about her engagement?

9. What does Waverly realize during their conversation?

10. Where will Waverly and Rich travel for their honeymoon?

Answers

1. Waverly wants to announce her engagement to Rich Schields.

2. She ignores it.

3. Lindo returns to her old self when Waverly has chicken pox.

4. Waverly is afraid that Lindo will find a real flaw that will affect Waverly's feelings for Rich.

5. Marvin is Waverly's first husband and Shoshana's father.

6. When she thanks Suyuan for dinner, she adds that Rich said it was the best Chinese food he had ever eaten. She knows Suyuan will repeat this to Lindo and that Lindo will want to prove that she is the better cook.

7. Rich brings French wine and drinks too much of it; he uses chopsticks and drops his food into his lap; he eats too much of some things and not enough of others; he criticizes Lindo's cooking by pouring soy sauce all over the serving platter; he addresses Waverly's parents with the wrong name and too informally.

8. She tells her the day after the dinner party.

9. Waverly realizes she has been hiding needlessly from her mother for years.

10. They will honeymoon in China.

Suggested Essay Topics

1. What references to chess maneuvers delineate the relationship between Waverly and Lindo in this story?

2. Compare and contrast Waverly's version of her argument with Lindo with Lindo's version in "Rules of the Game."

Without Wood

New Character:

Old Mr. Chou: *the Chinese equivalent of the Sandman*

Summary

When Rose was little, she had bad dreams. In one of them, she fell through a hole in Old Mr. Chou's floor into a garden. When he shouted at her, she began to run through fields of surrealistic flowers until she came upon sandboxes, each containing a new doll. An-mei told Old Mr. Chou that she knew which one Rose would select, so Rose deliberately chose a different one. An-mei shouted, "Stop her!" and Rose ran off, followed by Old Mr. Chou, who told her she should listen to her mother. When Rose told her the dream, An-mei laughed and said Rose should ignore Old Mr. Chou and just listen to her; Rose protests that even Old Mr. Chou listens to her.

The story jumps to the present. Rose meets An-mei at a funeral one month after telling her that she and Ted are getting a divorce. An-mei talks during most of the service, telling Rose she is too thin, asking her if she has money, asking her why Ted has sent a check, deciding that Ted "is doing monkey business with someone else." Rose disagrees with the last statement. An-mei asks why Rose can talk to a psychiatrist, but not to her, about her problems. She says a mother knows what is inside her children and that psychiatrists "only make you *hulihudu*, make you see *heimongmong*." The English equivalents are "confused" and "dark fog." The terms mean the sensation of being frightened and in the dark while trying to find the way. That is how she has felt lately, because she has been talking to everyone but Ted.

Ted sends divorce papers for her to sign and a check to help her out until the settlement. Rose is hurt because the pen he used to write the check was her gift to him last Christmas. He had promised he would only use it for "important things." Rose doesn't know what to do, so she puts the papers and the check "in a drawer where I kept store coupons which I never threw away and which I never used either."

Just before she pulls the papers out of the drawer to sign them, she thinks about how much she loves her house. She remembers that Ted used to pay careful attention to the garden. As she looks at it through a window, she notices that the garden has been neglected and wonders when Ted stopped working in it. She remembers a fortune she once read from a cookie: "When a husband stops paying attention to the garden, he's thinking of pulling up roots."

Three days later Ted calls. He is annoyed that Rose hasn't cashed his check or signed the papers and threatens to have them formally served. He wants the house; he wants to get remarried. Rose is stunned. She asks Ted to come over the next day, promising him the papers.

The next day she shows him the overgrown garden and says she likes it that way. She gives him his papers, and he offers to let her live in the house 30 days until she finds someplace else to live. Rose says she's staying in the house and that her lawyer will be serving him with papers. She has not signed his.

Rose tells Ted, "You can't just pull me out of your life and throw me away." She sees by his expression that he is *hulihudu* and that her words have power. That night she dreams that she is in the garden with Old Mr. Chou and her mother. It is foggy, and they are planting something in the planter boxes. When she walks closer, she can see freshly planted weeds "below the *heimongmong*, all along the ground...spilling out over the edges, running wild in every direction."

Analysis

Rose, who never had to make a decision before, now finds herself facing several. Amy Tan uses the situation to develop two intertwining themes. The first might be stated simply as "Listen to your mother." The second theme affirms the value of Chinese thinking in a multicultural society. The common denominator for the themes is An-mei.

The title refers to the Chinese belief that people consisted of fire, water, earth, metal, and wood. An imbalance of even one element could have serious consequences, as suggested in "The Red Candle," when the matchmaker says Lindo was unable to conceive because she had too much metal. In "The Joy Luck Club" Jing-mei says that An-mei had too little wood and was therefore unable to think for herself. In this story An-mei states that Rose has no wood, and, in an irony apparent only to the reader, confides that she herself almost became that way once. An-mei uses the analogy of a tree and a weed to explain the difference between having and not having wood and promises that a girl who listens to her mother will be strong.

"I used to believe everything my mother said," Rose says in the opening line of the story, "even when I didn't know what she meant." The children of immigrant parents usually reject their parents' culture and adopt the ways of the new country as they try to assimilate, and Rose fits the pattern. Forced to choose between American ways and Chinese ways, Rose chooses the American ways almost every time. "It was only later that I discovered there was a serious flaw with the American version," Rose asserts. "There were too many choices, so it was easy to get confused and pick the wrong thing." Again Rose fits the pattern of immigrants' children not appreciating their parents' culture until they are older.

An-mei suspects Ted is having an affair when she learns he has sent Rose a check. Rose finds the idea laughable at the time, but later she discovers her mother was right. At that point she abandons her American ideas in favor of her mother's Chinese ideas, decides she will speak to Ted, and invites him over. She retrieves the divorce papers from the drawer where she puts things she can't decide about, and finds her voice: "You can't just pull me out of your life and throw me away."

Rose's remark alludes to An-mei's analogy. She will not allow Ted to treat her like a weed. She has listened to her mother and has wood now. Ted is confused, *hulihudu*, by the power of her words; and Rose is pleased. Once the power of her mother's words had shaped her life, but Rose finally has power in words of her own. The incident underscores the twin themes.

The weeds in the garden represent Rose. An-mei's earlier description of weeds "running along the ground until someone pulls you out and throws you away" foreshadows Ted's intentions. Rose notices some weeds that have worked their way into cracks in the patio and under loose shingles and can't be pulled out without structural damage. The image suggests that Rose herself won't be discarded easily. She tells Ted she likes the garden overgrown and wild. Her defiance suggests her new strength.

The fog of the garden that afternoon parallels the *hulihudu*, confusion, Rose sees in Ted's face after this announcement. It returns in Rose's final dream, where planter boxes replace sandboxes and lovingly tended weeds "below the *heimongmong*" replace the dolls of her first dream. This image suggests that Rose can accept herself as she is.

Study Questions

1. Who is Old Mr. Chou?

2. What does An-mei suspect of Ted?

3. What do *hulihudu* and *heimongmong* mean?

4. How does Rose's psychiatrist respond to her feelings?

5. Why is Rose hurt when Ted sends her a check for $10,000?

6. According to An-mei, how can a girl become as strong as a tree?

7. According to Rose, what is the flaw with American ideas?

8. What clue suggests to Rose that Ted had been planning to leave her?

9. Why is Ted in a hurry to get the divorce over with?

10. Who does Rose see in her dream at the end of the story?

Answers

1. The guardian to the gate of dreams, Old Mr. Chou is the equivalent of the Sandman.

2. An-mei thinks Ted is having an affair.

3. *Hulihudu* means "confused"; *heimongmong* means "dark fog." They imply troubled feelings and not knowing where to turn for help.

4. He seems sleepy and bored; he does not offer any help or insight.

5. Ted wrote the check with a pen that was a gift from Rose. He said he would only use it for important papers.

6. An-mei says she must listen to her mother.

7. American ideas allow too many choices.

8. Ted had neglected the garden where he used to spend hours.

9. Ted wants to remarry.

10. Rose sees Old Mr. Chou and her mother.

Suggested Essay Topics

1. In what ways does this story use the motif of weeds?

2. In what ways does this story validate the theme of "listen to your mother"?

Best Quality

Summary

Jing-mei, the narrator, describes a pendant necklace Suyuan gave her a few weeks before her death. Called a "life's importance," the pendant is an elaborately carved piece of white and green jade about the size of her little finger. She believes the carvings symbolize her mother's wishes for her, but she doesn't know what they are, and no one else can tell her.

The story flashes back to the night her mother gave her the pendant. Suyuan had invited the Jongs over to celebrate Chinese New Year, so earlier in the day she and Jing-mei went shopping for crabs. As Jing-mei selects the tenth crab, she accidentally causes another crab to lose a leg. The manager sees them and forces them to buy the extra crab.

At dinner each person takes the best of the crabs left, until the platter reaches Jing-mei. She starts to take the one with the missing leg, offering the better one to her mother. Suyuan insists that Jing-mei take the good one. As the others eat, Suyuan quietly takes her crab into the kitchen.

The dinner conversation is friendly and lively until Waverly asks Jing-mei if she isn't afraid to have her hair cut by a gay beautician. After more insults, Jing-mei decides to embarrass Waverly. She asks when Waverly's firm will pay for some free-lance copywriting she had done more than a month ago. Everyone grows quiet. Waverly tells June that her writing was not good enough. Jing-mei stammers that of course revision is at no cost. Waverly says that Jing-mei's work is unsophisticated and has no style. She mocks it, repeating it as a television announcer would, and everyone laughs. Jing-mei picks up a couple of plates, trying not to cry.

After everyone has left, Suyuan comes into the kitchen and starts to make tea as Jing-mei puts away the dishes. When Jing-mei asks why Suyuan didn't eat her crab, Suyuan answers that it was a bad crab. What if someone else had chosen it? she wonders. Suyuan smiles. "Only *you* pick that crab. Nobody else take it. I already know this. Everybody else want best quality. You thinking different." It sounds like a compliment.

Jing-mei asks Suyuan why she didn't use the new dishes, her gift five years ago. Suyuan replies she forgot she had them. Then, as if she had just remembered, she gives Jing-mei the necklace she is wearing. When Jing-mei protests, Suyuan insists, saying she had meant to give it to her long ago. Jing-mei accuses Suyuan of giving her the necklace because of the scene with Waverly. Suyuan dismisses the idea, saying Waverly is like a crab that always walks sideways or crooked. Jing-mei, she says, goes a different way.

Analysis

"Best Quality" moves easily between discussion of best quality things and best quality people, emphasizing that life's importance lies in showing respect to others and to oneself.

Suyuan buys crab, a delicacy, to celebrate the Chinese New Year. She wants to offer her guests the best, so when she is forced to purchase the one with the missing leg, she considers it an extra, not one of the ten she needs. She is not expecting Shoshana, a child, to eat crab. Waverly, however, gives the biggest and best crab to her daughter, even though she knows Shoshana doesn't like it. Like every other mother, Waverly wants her daughter to have the best.

As the platter goes around, the guests each choose the best for themselves except Jing-mei, who offers the better one to her mother. Suyuan, like Waverly, insists that her daughter have the best, even though she knows Jing-mei doesn't care for crab and even though she believes the crab she gives herself is not fit to eat. Both Jing-mei and Suyuan offer the best to others and are willing to take second-best for themselves.

Suyuan says of the pendant she gives Jing-mei, "Not so good, this jade." She offers hope for its future, though, saying it will become greener if Jing-mei wears it every day. Jade symbolizes purity, in this case purity of intention: Mother and daughter share a willingness to offer their best to others, which is more important than having the best quality possessions.

Some critics have suggested that Suyuan's words to Jing-mei in the kitchen are in the nature of a gentle scolding, that Jing-mei has never wanted the best for herself, a pattern introduced in "Two Kinds" when she refused to develop her musical talent. The necklace suggests that Suyuan wants her daughter to remember that she is "still worth something." The gift follows Jing-mei's vision of herself as a success only at small things. No doubt her mother's vote of confidence is welcome.

Several critics have commented on the final scene in this story, in which Jing-mei takes her mother's place in the kitchen, symbolically becoming her mother. Throughout literature daughters have identified with their mothers hesitantly or uncertainly. Jing-mei, however, is quite comfortable in assuming some of her mother's role, suggesting that she has found strength in her mother's confidence and love. She will need that strength when she travels to China to tell her sisters about Suyuan.

Study Questions

1. What is a life's importance?

2. Why does Jing-mei shop with her mother in Chinatown?

3. What complaints does Suyuan have against her tenants? What complaints do they have against her?

4. Why does Suyuan tell Jing-mei to put the eleventh crab back in the tank? Why do they buy it?

5. Waverly gives Shoshana the best crab on the platter. How does Shoshana react?

6. The party is ruined when Waverly and Jing-mei argue. What do they argue about, and who starts it?

7. Why doesn't Suyuan use the dishes Jing-mei gave her?

8. How does Suyuan describe Waverly?

9. Why is Jing-mei fixing her father a spicy dish?

10. In what ways does Jing-mei show she identifies with her mother rather than competes with her?

Answers

1. It is a jade pendant that is elaborately carved with symbols.

2. They are buying crabs for that night's Chinese New Year dinner.

3. Suyuan says the tenants use too much water, sometimes bathing twice a day, and that they put out too much garbage. The tenants claim that Suyuan poisoned their cat.

4. The eleventh crab is missing a leg, and that is bad luck on Chinese New Year. The manager makes them buy it because they are responsible for the missing leg.

5. Shoshana whines that she doesn't like crab.

6. The argument starts when Waverly implies that Jing-mei's beautician might have AIDS and that Jing-mei goes to him because it's all she can afford. Then they argue about what to do with her advertising copy, which Waverly says isn't good enough for their firm.

7. Suyuan says she forgot she had them. She was saving them for a special occasion.

8. During dinner Suyuan says Waverly was born sophisticated. Afterwards she says Waverly is like a crab that always walks sideways and crooked.

9. Suyuan believed spicy foods restore the spirit and good health. Jing-mei enjoys fixing this particular dish, and her father likes it.

10. In the final scene she takes her mother's place in her kitchen. She has the same complaints as Suyuan about the tenants' using too much water. She fixes a meal for her father. She tries to shoo the cat away and is equally unsuccessful.

Suggested Essay Topics

1. After Waverly insults Jing-mei several times, Suyuan says to Waverly, "True, cannot teach style. June not sophisticate like you. Must be born this way." Explain this apparent betrayal in light of Suyuan's later contempt for Waverly.

2. Suyuan says she knew that only Jing-mei would choose the bad crab. She says, "Everyone else want best quality. You thinking different." Is this a compliment or a scolding? Defend your answer.

3. Suyuan gives Jing-mei a gift of jade that she admits is not the best quality. Compare this necklace with Lindo's gold bracelets in "The Red Candle." Can we draw conclusions about the two women based on the attitudes surrounding these items?

Queen Mother of the Western Skies

Vignette

Summary

A grandmother plays with her infant granddaughter on her lap. She says she doesn't know which is better, innocence or safety. She was once innocent and laughed "for no reason" but gave up that foolishness to protect herself. She taught her daughter to do the same. Now she wonders if she did the right thing.

The baby laughs. The grandmother pretends the baby is Syi Wang Mu, the Queen Mother of the Western Skies, who has already lived many lifetimes and knows the answer. She listens, and thanks the baby for her advice. She says the baby must teach its mother, the grandmother's daughter, "how to lose your innocence but not your hope. How to laugh forever."

Analysis

This vignette completes the cycle. In the first vignette, a young woman travels to America with a swan and dreams. In the second, the woman, now the mother of a young child, struggles to raise her. In the third, her daughter is an adult, but she still tries to help her. In this vignette the woman is a grandmother. She reflects on her life and wonders whether she has done the best she could for her daughter. She decides that the best way to raise children is to show them the evils of the world but to maintain the hope that life can be good despite evil.

Maintaining hope in the face of the realities of life is one of the most important themes of this novel.

Study Questions

1. Who are the two characters in this vignette?

2. What reason does the grandmother give for the baby's laughter?

3. What is the relationship between the grandmother and the baby's mother?

4. Why had the grandmother given up her innocence?

5. Why might the grandmother wonder if she has done the right thing?

6. Who is Syi Wang Mu?

7. Why would Syi Wang Mu know the answer to the grandmother's question?

8. Who else needs to know this answer?

9. What will people be able to do as long as they still have hope, according to this vignette?

10. In what way does this vignette differ from the other three?

Answers

1. The two characters are the grandmother and her granddaughter.

2. The grandmother says Buddha is teaching her to laugh for no reason. She also says the baby is free and innocent.

3. The grandmother is the mother of the baby's mother.

4. The grandmother needed to protect herself from the evils of the world. To do that, she had to gain experience. She could not go through life blindly.

5. The grandmother knows that her daughter will raise this baby the same way she was raised.

6. Syi Wang Mu is the Queen Mother of the Western Skies.

7. Syi Wang Mu has lived forever, through many lifetimes.

8. The baby's mother, the grandmother's daughter, needs to know this answer.

9. They will always be able to laugh.

10. In this vignette the grandmother learns from the child, instead of the other way around.

Suggested Essay Topics

1. In what ways has the novel already shown characters who lost their innocence but not their hope?

2. In this vignette, the grandmother learns from her grand-daughter and plans to share that learning with her daughter, the baby's mother. What does this cycling of wisdom suggest about generations learning from one another?

Magpies

New Characters:

Wu Tsing: *An-mei's mother's second husband, a wealthy merchant in Tientsin*

Yan Chang: *An-mei's mother's personal servant*

First Wife: *Wu Tsing's official wife, mother of two daughters. She is addicted to opium*

Second Wife: *Wu Tsing's concubine. She dominates the other women in the household*

Third Wife: *Wu Tsing's concubine. She has three daughters*

Fifth Wife: *Wu Tsing's most recent concubine. She is very young*

Syaudi: *son of Wu Tsing and An-mei's mother. Second Wife claims him as her own*

Summary

An-mei, the narrator, talks about Rose's divorce. Rose complains that she has no choice in the matter, but An-mei says refusing to make an effort is a choice. An-mei's Chinese upbringing trained her to want nothing for herself. She tried to raise Rose differently, but "she came out the same way!" An-mei wonders if it's just because they're all women.

The story flashes back to when An-mei is nine, and her mother returns to the family home in Ningpo. She is not welcome. She mourns the death of her mother, Popo, even though Popo had disowned her years earlier. After Popo's funeral, she prepares to leave. An-mei leaves with her.

During the long trip to Wu Tsing's, An-mei's mother points out that An-mei will have a new home, new family, and many new things. Every night An-mei falls asleep snuggled next to her mother. She feels very comfortable.

When Wu Tsing and the other wives return, everything changes. Yan Chang tells An-mei the circumstances allowing Second Wife to manipulate Wu Tsing easily. She also relates why An-mei's mother married him. These revelations cause An-mei to view the household dynamic from an adult perspective. When her mother later commits suicide, An-mei understands both the causes and the intended effect. She gains the life her mother wanted for her and Syaudi, her son.

The story returns to the present. An-mei understands confusion and powerlessness, but she refuses to submit. A village that fought off birds that had destroyed their crops for generations represents that courage to her.

Analysis

An-mei's story concludes with her observation that women have more choices in America today than they had in China in her childhood. An-mei herself participates in the transition between the two. She stops submitting, swallowing her tears, and begins asserting herself, shouting.

Amy Tan uses both swallowing tears and shouting as motifs to underscore this progression. Early in the story An-mei's mother tells her daughter how disappointed she was when Popo told her it was time to grow up, to stop shouting, playing, and crying. She learned that women should swallow their tears so they don't let their sorrow cause others to be happy. Thus, women were denied the expression of even basic emotions. Men could shout, as An-mei's uncle does; but women were not permitted to respond in kind. An-mei's

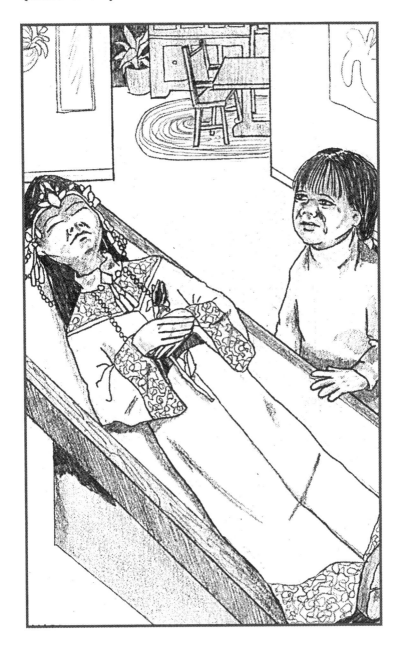

mother kneels before him instead, "crying with her mouth closed," completely powerless. An-mei's decision to leave with her mother is a silent defiance of his wishes.

When Wu Tsing acknowledges his debt to her mother, An-mei sees another opportunity to assert herself. She begins to shout, noisily claiming power. Years later the story of the villagers shouting to defeat the predatory birds causes her to shout for joy. The transition from vulnerability to strength is complete.

In addition to these two motifs, three symbols in this story deserve mention. An-mei describes the elaborate European clock in her mother's room. The figures go through their routines when the clock chimes the hour. At first An-mei is fascinated by its intricacy. Later it becomes a nuisance, keeping her awake at night. Eventually she learns to ignore it and discovers that she has developed the ability to disregard "something meaningless calling to me." Recognizing and resisting the meaningless things is a measure of An-mei's developing ability to recognize what is true.

An-mei learns the lesson a second time when Second Wife gives her the necklace. Once her mother demonstrates that it is glass, she sees it as "something meaningless." Once we learn of Second Wife's earlier treachery, the purpose of the necklace becomes evident: to buy An-mei's loyalty. The ring of watery blue sapphire that An-mei's mother gives her at the end of this lesson is the same ring An-mei throws into the cove to bring back Bing in "Half and Half."

The final symbol serves as a foreshadowing. When An-mei's mother gives her a Western outfit to wear from the steamer to Wu Tsing's home, nothing fits. Tan points especially to the white shoes, which have to be stuffed with paper before An-mei can wear them. She mentions twice that she has trouble walking in these shoes, a suggestion that she will have difficulty following in her mother's footsteps in the household of Wu Tsing. Her efforts to assert herself are the result of her mother's actions, but the opposite of them as well. She does not swallow her tears; she shouts.

Tan frames the story of An-mei's childhood with reference to Rose and her divorce, an ongoing plot from "Half and Half" and "Without Wood." Rose believes she has no choices, but Rose does not know what it means to have no choices. An-mei does, and she shouts for joy that the change has come.

Study Questions

1. What do magpies represent?

2. The turtle tells An-mei's mother to swallow her tears. What was the turtle's reason?

3. Who is Yan Chang?

4. At first, An-mei is very happy at Wu Tsing's. What factors contribute to her happiness?

5. An-mei describes the clock in her mother's room in great detail and says she learned something from it. What did she learn?

6. Why does An-mei's mother break one of the pearls in the necklace Second Wife gives An-mei?

7. How had Second Wife arranged for An-mei's mother to become Wu Tsing's fourth wife?

8. What weakness of Wu Tsing does Second Wife exploit?

9. Who is Syaudi?

10. Why was the timing of An-mei's mother's suicide so important?

Answers

1. Magpies are birds of joy.

2. The turtle said one person's sadness makes another person happy.

3. Yan Chang is An-mei's mother's personal servant. She helps take care of An-mei.

4. An-mei is happy because she is with her mother, because she is surrounded by new and amazing things, and because she is living amid great wealth.

5. She learned not to pay attention to meaningless things.

6. An-mei's mother wants An-mei to see Second Wife as the fraud she is. She does not want An-mei to give her loyalty to the woman who has caused so much pain.

7. First she invited An-mei's mother for dinner. The next night she invited her to play mah jong and then to stay the night. During the night she left the bed they were sharing and let Wu Tsing in. After he raped An-mei's mother, Second Wife spread the rumor that An-mei's mother had seduced him. No one else would have anything to do with her, so she was forced to marry him.

8. Second Wife knows that Wu Tsing is afraid of ghosts. Whenever she pretends she is about to become one, she gets what she wants.

9. Syaudi is An-mei's half brother, the son of her mother and Wu Tsing. Second Wife, however, has claimed him as her own.

10. The Chinese believed a dead person's ghost returns on the third day after death. The ghost of a woman can get revenge for a bad marriage by destroying the man's good fortune. They also believed all debts must be paid on the first day of the lunar new year. By making sure that she died two days before the lunar new year, An-mei's mother makes Wu Tsing acutely aware of the debt he owes her, a debt he can repay only by treating An-mei and Syaudi with great respect. He promises to raise them as if they were the children of First Wife and to revere her as if she had been First Wife. In doing this, he elevates both An-mei and Syaudi to a status above Second Wife, a position An-mei exploits at once.

Suggested Essay Topics

1. An-mei says she learned to shout the day Wu Tsing promised to treat her as if she were the daughter of First Wife. She also says she shouted for joy when the Chinese peasants defeated the birds that had plagued them. Where else does the story mention shouting? What does it add? Trace the development of the motif of shouting in this story.

2. An-mei's mother is Fourth Wife, *Sz Tai* in Chinese. An-mei says that "sz" sounds like "die" if said incorrectly. In what ways is this an appropriate name for her?

Waiting Between the Trees

New Character:

Ying-ying's first husband: *never named, Ying-ying called him "Uncle" when she first met him. He is murdered by a mistress*

Summary

Ying-ying, the narrator, loves her daughter Lena, but they have never been close. She wants to tell her daughter everything about her life now in an effort to rescue Lena from herself.

The story flashes back to Ying-ying's childhood. She says she was a wild, stubborn, and arrogant girl from a wealthy family. She met a coarse, drunken man the night her youngest aunt was married. The day after her aunt's wedding, she saw a sign that convinced her she would marry him.

As they sat in a boat on Tai Lake not long after their marriage, Ying-ying fell in love with him and began to do everything just for him. She knew she was pregnant with a boy the night it happened, and she was very happy.

She began to worry when she noticed her husband taking more frequent and longer business trips, especially after she was pregnant. Eventually her youngest aunt told her he was living with an opera singer in the North. Even later she learned there had been many other women. In her grief and anger at being abandoned, she had an abortion. Ying-ying remarks ironically that Lena thinks she doesn't know "what it means to not want a baby."

Ying-ying was born in the year of the Tiger, and her tiger spirit helped her overcome adversity. The tiger's colors symbolize its two sides: The gold side is powerful and active; the black side is shrewd and patient. She learned to be patient after her husband left her. Overcome by depression, she left her mother-in-law's home and moved in with some cousins in the country outside Shanghai. She lived in crowded, dirty conditions for 10 years. Then she moved to the city and got a job selling women's clothing.

Clifford St. Clair, an American clothing importer, introduced himself one day. Ying-ying found him unremarkable, but she also knew he was a sign that her life was about to change again.

Four years later a letter from her aunt told her that her husband was dead. Ying-ying "decided to let Saint marry [her]." She put aside her own spirit, her *chi*, because it had only brought her pain and describes herself as "a tiger that neither pounced nor lay waiting between the trees. I became an unseen spirit." She came to America with him and raised a daughter with whom she did not feel close. She didn't care, because she had no spirit. She can't say she didn't love her husband, but she says "it was the love of a ghost."

Ying-ying wants to give Lena her tiger spirit, because, to Ying-ying's shame, Lena has no *chi*. She can hear Lena and Harold talking downstairs. She knows that once she knocks over the vase and table, Lena will come upstairs. She says, "Her eyes will see nothing in the darkness, where I am waiting between the trees."

Analysis

The image that unites this story is that of the tiger. Ying-ying was born in 1914, a year of the Tiger. Her husband fills out her paperwork incorrectly when she enters the United States, we are told in "The Voice from the Wall," but that does not change her from a Tiger to a Dragon.

According to the Chinese zodiac, which runs on a 12-year cycle, tigers have great courage. They are sensitive, emotional, kind to their friends, and capable of great love. They can also be mean and stubborn, and they do not trust easily. Many of these qualities describe Ying-ying.

As a child Ying-ying might be characterized as living in the golden, or yang, side of the tiger because she is very active. As a young woman she stubbornly believes she is too good for any one man. When she falls in love with her first husband, however, every action she takes is designed to please him.

When he abandons her for another, Ying-ying aborts his son. Here the reader learns the background for Ying-ying's statement in "The Voice from the Wall" that the loss of her second son was her fault partly because "I had given no thought to killing my other son!" The years spent in the country may be seen as living in the black, yin, side of her tiger, passive and patient.

When the news of her first husband's death comes 14 years later, she decides to marry Clifford St. Clair, whom she calls "Saint."

To do that, she says, "I willingly gave up my *chi*, the spirit that caused me so much pain."

Chi describes not only force of personality, but also a sense of self-worth. When Ying-ying suppresses hers, Lena has no model to learn from. As a result both women are manipulated by their husbands without protest in "Rice Husband," one linguistically and one financially. Ying-ying feels responsible that Lena will not speak up for herself. Before she dies, Ying-ying wants to pass on her *chi*, a final gift to Lena.

In the closing scene, she summons the pain she has avoided to fashion a metaphoric weapon. Lena, born in 1950 and also a Tiger, will resist her mother because she does not see what Ying-ying sees. The end of "Rice Husband" suggests that Lena is beginning to see that change is needed, however, so the reader is hopeful for both women's sakes.

Study Questions

1. When Ying-ying wore her hair down, what did her mother say she looked like?

2. Ying-ying did not appreciate what she had as a child. What object best symbolizes that statement?

3. When did Ying-ying's husband's business trips start becoming longer and more frequent?

4. How did Ying-ying feel about her pregnancy?

5. What do the two colors of the tiger symbolize?

6. Although Ying-ying did not throw herself into the lake after her husband left her, in what ways did she become like one of the lady ghosts of the lake?

7. Where did Ying-ying meet Clifford St. Clair?

8. How did Ying-ying's first husband die?

9. What aspect of Lena causes Ying-ying to be ashamed?

10. What does Ying-ying do to summon her *chi* and bring both her black and gold sides back?

Answers

1. Her mother said Ying-ying looked like a "lady ghost at the bottom of the lake," a woman who became pregnant without being married and drowned herself to hide her shame. Later, her ghost would haunt the homes of living people with her hair undone.

2. A jade cigarette jar symbolizes her lack of appreciation. She took it, threw away the cigarettes, and played in the mud with it.

3. He was gone more after she became pregnant.

4. She was very happy at first, but after her husband abandoned her, she was so angry that she had an abortion and told the nurses to throw the baby into the lake.

5. The black represents yin—patient and cunning. The gold is yang—powerful and forceful.

6. Ying-ying was very depressed. She covered her mirrors so she could not see her grief; she left her hair down because she was too weak to pin it up; and she went to live with some cousins in the country, where she did nothing for 10 years.

7. They met in Shanghai where she worked in a dress shop.

8. When he tried to leave his last mistress, she stabbed him with a sharp knife.

9. Ying-ying is ashamed that Lena has no spirit, no *chi*.

10. Ying-ying remembers the events of her life that have caused her pain. She must accept the pain rather than hide from it in order to regain her spirit.

Suggested Essay Topics

1. Ying-ying was born in the year of the Tiger. In what ways is the Tiger a good symbol for her?

2. What evidence suggests that Ying-ying lost both her innocence and her hope as a result of her first marriage?

Double Face

New Characters:

Lindo's helper in Peking: *never named, she gives Lindo advice about coming to America*

Lindo's helper in San Francisco: *never named, she helps Lindo get an apartment and job*

Summary

Lindo narrates this story, set in the present. Waverly has second thoughts about going to China on her honeymoon with Rich. Lindo assures her that everyone in China will know she is not Chinese by the look on her face.

Lindo wanted her children to have "the best combination: American circumstances and Chinese character." She did not realize that the two don't mix. She was able to teach Waverly the American part about opportunity but not the Chinese part about personal integrity.

Lindo and Waverly are at Mr. Rory's, having Lindo's hair styled. When Mr. Rory mentions that Lindo and Waverly look alike, Lindo tells Waverly a person can see someone's character and future in their facial features.

Lindo recalls coming to America. She had paid a woman to advise her on how to deal with American immigration officials and how to complete paperwork. The woman had also given her the address of someone in San Francisco's Chinatown who would help her after she arrived. The woman in Chinatown charged Lindo $3.00 for a hastily jotted list of addresses. Lindo used the list to find an apartment and a job in a fortune cookie factory, where she made a friend, An-mei Hsu.

An-mei introduced Lindo to Tin Jong. At first Lindo objected to An-mei's introducing her to someone from a different region of China, but An-mei pointed out that, in America, "everybody is now from the same village even if they come from different parts of China." Because Lindo and Tin spoke different dialects of Chinese, they couldn't really speak to each other. They attended English class together, and sometimes wrote in Chinese. Lindo was sure Tin

really liked her, though, because he would act out what he was trying to say. Lindo used a carefully planted fortune cookie to let Tin know she wanted to marry him. Nine months after their marriage their first child, Winston, was born.

When Waverly was born, Lindo started thinking about things differently. She wanted everything to be better for her daughter. She named her after the street they lived on because she wanted Waverly to know she belonged somewhere. She also realized that one day her daughter would move away "and take a piece of me with [her]."

The story returns to the present, as Mr. Rory puts the finishing touches on Lindo's hair. Lindo compares her reflection to her daughter's and notices Waverly's nose is crooked. Waverly says it has always been this way, just like Lindo's; and she likes it. It makes them both look devious.

Lindo remembers that when she returned to China last year, everyone could tell she was a foreigner. She wonders what she has lost and gained, and decides she will ask Waverly's opinion.

Analysis

The title "Double Face" returns the reader to the motif of yin and yang, which dominates the novel. In this story, however, more attention is placed on the search for balance between the two. The title works on several levels, suggesting the duality of Lindo and Waverly, of American circumstances and Chinese character, of Lindo's "American face," which hides her thoughts, and her "Chinese face," which is sincere, and even the duality of a straight nose and a crooked one.

One of the important images in this story is the reflection in the hairdresser's mirror. Waverly is a reflection of Lindo, and Lindo is proud of her. Lindo, on the other hand, will reflect on Waverly at the wedding; and Waverly is not proud of her. Lindo is disappointed. Reflection also serves as a metaphor as Lindo thinks about the events of her life before Waverly's birth.

When Mr. Rory remarks on how much the two women look alike, Lindo is pleased, but Waverly is not. The reader will recall that young women often resist identifying with their mothers from the discussion in "Best Quality." Waverly certainly fits that pattern. She refers to Lindo in the third person while she is present, for example, and asks her a question and then answers it herself. She does not treat her mother as she would treat anyone else she respects.

Lindo's reflection on the day her mother told her fortune by reading her face points indirectly to Waverly, too, since the two women look so much alike. Her mother warns that a twisted nose leads to bad luck. A woman who has a crooked nose, she says, "is always following the wrong things, the wrong people, the worst luck." Lindo's nose is straight until the bus accident, but Waverly's has always been crooked. She likes it, saying it makes both women look "devious," which she defines as "looking one way, while following another….We mean what we say, but our intentions are different…we're two-faced." As long as she gets what she wants, Waverly is happy to be two-faced.

This is a very un-Chinese way of thinking. Lindo has to get used to it. She remembers that, on her recent trip to China, everyone knew just by looking at her face that she was a foreigner. Lindo wonders what she has lost and gained from her American circumstances. In a move that suggests that she has come to value Waverly's opinion, she decides to ask her.

One of the strengths of this story is Lindo's voice summarizing her life. The author grants the older generation a respect that her character Waverly does not. The daughter will have the last word only because her mother values her opinion. The stories of the mothers do not end just because the daughters are adults. Wisdom continues to develop. In this sense Tan is using a Chinese character trait, respect, to illustrate American circumstances.

Study Questions

1. Waverly wonders whether she will look Chinese when she goes there on her honeymoon. Lindo assures her that everyone in China will know she is a foreigner. What will give her away?

2. Lindo wanted her children to have American circumstances and Chinese character. What was wrong with that?

3. Why has Waverly brought Lindo to Mr. Rory?

4. In what ways does Waverly show that she is ashamed of Lindo?

5. What kind of life did Lindo's mother predict on the basis of her facial features?

6. What made Lindo's nose change from being straight and smooth to crooked? What is wrong with having a crooked nose?

7. Who introduced Lindo and Tin?

8. Language is a barrier to Lindo and Tin at first. What problem does Lindo especially mention? How do they get around it?

9. Why did Lindo name her daughter after a street?

10. Lindo decides she will ask Waverly's opinion of what she has lost and gained in America. What does this decision tell us about their relationship?

Answers

1. Lindo says the way she walks and the expression on her face will give her away, even if her clothing and makeup do not.

2. The two don't mix.

3. Waverly is marrying Rich, and she wants her mother to look nice.

4. She talks about Lindo in front of her, and she treats her as if she can't speak English, make her own decisions, or hear well.

5. She will recognize opportunity, have a long life without becoming a burden, and be clever; but she will also have troubles early in her life. She would be a good wife, mother, and daughter-in-law.

6. Lindo bumped her nose on a bus. A girl who has a crooked nose will also have troubles.

7. An-mei Hsu introduced them.

8. She and Tin can't tease or scold one another while they are dating because they speak different dialects of Chinese and both have poor English. She misses the teasing because that's how she could tell if the relationship were serious. They get around it by writing in Chinese and by acting out what they mean. Eventually they learn enough English and enough of each other's dialects to scold and tease.

9. Lindo wanted Waverly to know she belonged somewhere, so she named her after the street on which they lived.

10. Lindo has come to value Waverly's opinion. The reconciliation they began in "Four Directions" has apparently worked out.

Suggested Essay Topics

1. When Lindo mentions two faces, the reader may recognize a yin and yang. In this story, what pairs may be seeking balance?

2. You have read four stories about Lindo and Waverly: "The Red Candle," "Rules of the Game," "Four Directions," and "Double Face." Would you agree or disagree that Lindo's mother accurately predicted their lives and character by "reading" Lindo's face? Bear in mind that Lindo and Waverly look very much alike.

A Pair of Tickets

New Characters:

Aiyi: *Jing-mei's great-aunt*

Lili: *Aiyi's great-granddaughter*

Wang Chwun Yu and Wang Chwun Hwa: *Suyuan's twin daughters, Jing-mei's half sisters. Their names mean "Spring Rain" and "Spring Flower"*

Mei Ching and Mei Han: *the couple who find and raise the twins*

Suyuan's schoolmate: *never named. She recognizes the twins and contacts Suyuan with their address*

Summary

Jing-mei narrates this story. She and her father are on a train from Hong Kong to Shenzhen, China. Her father has tears in his eyes as he looks out the train window at the countryside. Even Jing-mei is moved by the sight, "as if [she] had seen this a long, long time ago, and had almost forgotten." After they visit Canning's aunt in Guangzhou, they will go to Shanghai to meet Jing-mei's twin half sisters, whom she has never seen before.

At Guangzhou Jing-mei and her father meet Aiyi, his aunt, and her family. The city seems very modern, and the taxi pulls up in front of an imposing hotel that doesn't fit Jing-mei's ideas of Communist China. The rooms are even stocked with Western snacks and drinks. The family decides just to stay at the hotel so they can visit.

At 1:00 a.m. Jing-mei wakes up, sitting on the floor in her hotel room. Everyone has gone to sleep except Aiyi and Canning, talking quietly about Suyuan's daughters. Jing-mei asks why her mother abandoned the twins.

Canning narrates this flashback. Suyuan walked several days, unable to get a ride. Eventually she could not walk any farther. Convinced she was going to die, she put the babies on the side of the road and lay down next to them, begging passers-by to take them. No one would.

When no one was left on the road, Suyuan put jewelry under one girl's shirt and money under the other's. She wrote a message on the backs of photos of her family, asking whoever found the girls to take care of them and take them to their family in Shanghai for a reward. She touched the girls on the cheek and left without looking back. Her only hope was that they would be found by someone who would take good care of them. She did not allow herself to envision any other alternative.

She walked a while, then fainted. She awoke to find she had been rescued by American missionaries who brought her to Chungking, where she learned that her husband had died two weeks earlier. She met Canning in the hospital there.

Mei Ching and her husband, Mei Han, who lived in a hidden cave, found the twins and raised them, since they had no children of their own. They discovered the valuables and photographs Suyuan had left, but neither of them could read. By the time they found someone who could tell them what was written on the photographs, Mei Ching didn't want to give them up.

When the girls were eight, Mei Han died. Mei Ching decided to take the girls back to their family, hoping she would be hired as their nanny. The address on the back of the pictures was now a factory, though, and no one knew anything about the family whose house had been at that site. Suyuan and Canning had returned to that address, too, seven years earlier, hoping to find her daughters and family.

When it was possible to send mail to China once again, Suyuan immediately began to write to her old friends, asking them to look for her daughters. Suyuan even contemplated going back to China, but Canning, not knowing her motives, told her they were too old for the trip. Canning wonders if perhaps Suyuan's spirit guided the friend from Shanghai who found the twins walking down the stairs in a department store not long after Suyuan died.

Jing-mei narrates as she and Canning say good-bye to Aiyi and her family at the airport, knowing they'll never meet again. Their plane lands in Shanghai. Someone shouts, "She's arrived!" and Jing-mei thinks she sees her mother. Then she sees the other sister. Both are waving, and one is holding the picture of her she sent them earlier. Once Jing-mei gets past the gate, they all hug.

Her sisters look familiar to her. She realizes that she is Chinese because her family is Chinese. As Suyuan had predicted, it was in her blood, "waiting to be let go."

Canning takes a Polaroid of the three women, and they stand together to watch it develop:

> The gray-green surface changes to the bright colors of our three images, sharpening and deepening all at once. And although we don't speak, I know we all see it: Together we look like our mother. Her same eyes, her same mouth, open in surprise to see, at last, her long-cherished wish.

Analysis

Jing-mei's trip to China serves as a metaphor for a journey into her perceptions about herself. She considers how she has viewed her sisters, China itself, her mother, and herself as Chinese.

Tan incorporates a subtle motif about age that points out not only Jing-mei's view of her sisters but also everyone else's assumptions about her. At first Jing-mei thinks of her sisters only as babies. When she discovers that they are alive, she pictures them first as six-year-olds and later as ten or eleven. Not until she imagines herself bringing them the news of Suyuan's death does she see them as adults. The motif resurfaces when Jing-mei meets Aiyi, her great-aunt. Aiyi's first word to her is *"Jandale,"* "So big already." Her sisters say something similar when she meets them at last: *"Meimei jandale,"* "Little sister has grown up." Other changes in vision also take place.

For example, Jing-mei says, "This is Communist China?" as she gets used to the idea of modern cities and traffic, luxurious Western-style hotels, and Western food. She expected China to be like the shampoo in the hotel, somehow inferior. Being Chinese is not what she thought it would be, either. In China Jing-mei does not look different from anyone else. In America she is separated from many people by appearance. Here, she fits right in.

During the trip Jing-mei also learns the rest of her mother's wartime story. She sees that her actions were justified. Suyuan's quixotic and necessary efforts to find the girls again ennoble her. The Dickensian coincidence of the girls' discovery becomes a forgivable device when matched with the tragedy of Suyuan's early death. Jing-mei sees her mother in a different light. In "The Joy Luck Club," she said she didn't know anything about her mother. By the time she meets her sisters, she has much to tell them.

The new perception of her mother leads Jing-mei to a new understanding of herself. From the generation before her father to the generation after her, she sees friendly, hardworking people who seem very typical to her. Her family is Chinese, and she does not have to resist the designation any longer. "It is so obvious…After all these years, it can finally be let go."

The meeting with her sisters, long anticipated in the novel, is anticlimactic. It serves more as a resolution to the conflicts Jing-mei and Suyuan experienced individually and together. As the women crowd around the Polaroid, a device Tan uses throughout the story, the reader sees Suyuan's strength and influence as surely as the three women see her physical characteristics. Her hope has become their joy and luck.

Study Questions

1. Why have Jing-mei and Canning gone to China?

2. Why did Lindo tell the twins that Suyuan would come to see them when Suyuan had been dead three months? Why did Jing-mei ask her to write a second letter?

3. How did Suyuan know that her entire family had been killed in the bombing?

4. What aspects of China surprise Jing-mei?

5. What does Jing-mei's name tell us about Suyuan's hopes?

6. Why had Suyuan abandoned her babies?

7. What happened to the girls after Suyuan left them?

8. Why did Canning refuse to come to China with Suyuan when she suggested it?

9. Why does the first sister remind Jing-mei of Suyuan?

10. What was Suyuan's long-cherished wish?

Answers

1. They will visit his aunt and her twin half sisters.

2. Lindo was reluctant to put such sad news in a letter; she said the twins should hear it from a member of their family. Jing-mei wanted her sisters to know before she arrived so that they wouldn't be disappointed and hate her and so that they wouldn't think Suyuan had died because of her neglect.

3. In the debris of the house Suyuan found a doll that a niece always carried with her. If the niece was in the house when the bomb fell, then her parents and the rest of the family must also have been there.

4. She is surprised that Guangzhou is a modern city, that an elegant hotel is so inexpensive, and that the room contains Western items such as German beer, Coke, and Cadbury's chocolate.

5. *Jing* means "essence" or "best quality." *Mei* means "little sister." She represents the essence of the other two sisters, a constant reminder that Suyuan hopes to see them again.

6. Suyuan thought she was about to die from dysentery, and she didn't want her babies to die with her.

7. They were adopted and raised by a childless couple who lived in caves not far from the road where Suyuan left them. Later they came to Shanghai.

8. Canning misunderstood what Suyuan wanted. He thought she just wanted to be a tourist.

9. The first sister has pressed her hand against her mouth the same way Suyuan did when Jing-mei crawled out from under the bed after being gone all afternoon.

10. Suyuan wanted to see all her daughters together.

Suggested Essay Topics

1. Why might Jing-mei want to hear the story of her mother's ordeal in Chinese rather than English?

2. Jing-mei does not understand what part of her is Chinese until she visits China and sees all the people that she is like. She is also like her American friends, but in a different way. Discuss what parts are American and what parts are Chinese.

Sample Analytical Paper Topics

Topic #1

One of the unifying images of the novel relates to the Daoist concept of yin and yang and seeking balance between the two. In what ways does the author make use of these images?

Outline

I.   Thesis Statement: *Author Amy Tan uses images of yin and yang to underscore the characters' search for balance.*

II.   Two sets of images characterize Rose.

    A.   In "Half and Half", "victim" and "hero" defines her relationship with Ted.

    B.   In "Without Wood" images of weeds and flowers reflect her struggle to choose between Chinese and American thinking.

III.   In "Waiting Between the Trees" Tan characterizes Ying-ying as a tiger, having both gold (yang) and black (yin) sides.

    A.   Her gold, active, yang side brings her pain.

    B.   Her black, passive, yin side protects her from pain, but also from joy.

    C.   She embraces her pain to pass on her *chi* on to Lena, who has no spirit.

IV. Lido acts as Waverly's "protective ally" but Waverly sees her as an opponent until they reconcile.

    A. In "Rules of the Game" Lindo supports Waverly as a chess player until Waverly shows she does not appreciate her help.

    B. In Four Directions" Waverly sees Lindo as her opponent.

    C. In "Double Face" Lindo respects Waverly as a source of advice.

V. In "A Pair of Tickets" Jing-mei (June) accepts both her American life and Chinese heritage.

    A. Until she goes to China, Jing-mei denies that she is Chinese.

    B. In China she realizes that she misunderstood what "be ing Chinese" is and understands that her family is Chinese.

VI. Conclusion: The pursuit of balance teaches, as the grandmother tells her granddaughter in the final vignette, "how to lose your innocence but not your hope. How to laugh forever."

Topic #2

One of the unusual features of this novel is its narrative technique. Tan uses 10 different narrators in 20 stories and vignettes spanning 2 continents and at least 73 years. The result, however, is a coherent whole. What devices make this possible?

Outline

I. Thesis Statement: *Author Amy Tan uses vignettes, allusions among stories, and ongoing conflicts to add unity to the novel.*

II. The vignettes add unity.

    A. Each vignette defines the basis for the next four stories.

    B. Together the vignettes describe the life cycle.

    C. The final vignette suggests a theme for the entire novel.

III.   Allusions among stories add unity.

    A.   An-mei's sapphire ring

    B.   Ying-ying's first son

    C.   Lindo's *chang*

    D.   Suyuan's twins

IV.   Ongoing conflicts add unity.

    A.   Suyuan and Lindo's friendly rivalry

    B.   Ying-ying's traumas

    C.   Lindo and Waverly's chess maneuvers

    D.   Jing-mei's understanding of who she is

V.   Conclusion: The narrative technique in *The Joy Luck Club* uses dissimilar elements to create an effective whole.

Topic #3

One of the dominant themes of twentieth-century American literature has been the search to define the self. This search has variously explored the influence of history, economics, religion, family, gender, and ethnicity. Characters must reconcile themselves with these forces before they are able to face the future. In what ways do the daughters in *The Joy Luck Club* come to terms with these influences?

Outline

I.   Thesis Statement: *Waverly Jong, Rose Hsu Jordan, Lena St. Clair, and Jing-mei Woo alternately resist and embrace their identities as daughters, as women, and as Chinese.*

II.   Waverly resists and embraces her identity as Lindo's daughter.

    A.   In "Rules of the Game" and "Four Directions" she rejects Lindo's pride in her.

    B.   By the end of "Four Directions" she no longer sees her mother as an adversary; she even contemplates taking Lindo along on her honeymoon.

III. Rose resists and embraces her self-concept as a woman of power.

A. In "Half and Half" she surrenders her will to Ted.

B. In the garden in "Without Wood" she asserts herself by announcing she intends to contest the divorce and remain in her home.

IV. Lena resists and embraces her understanding of herself as a woman of value.

A. In "Rice Husband" she allows Harold to take advantage of her love and generosity because she is afraid of losing him.

B. She begins to stand up to him by suggesting they re-evaluate their marriage.

V. Jing-mei (June) resists and embraces her identity as Chinese.

A. As a child she thinks Chinese means "strange and inferior."

B. Meeting her family in China teaches her that "Chinese" means "modern, friendly, and caring."

VI. Conclusion: As each character comes to terms with who she is, she affirms her mother's example of strength and courage.

Chinese Words and Expressions in the Novel

chang—a necklace of red jade

chi (pronounced "chee")—literally "breath," a person's spirit, self-respect, assertiveness

Ching! Ching!—Please, eat!

chuming—insight

Chunwang chihan—"If the lips are gone, the teeth will be cold," or, one thing is always the result of another.

dajya—the entire family

dyansyin—special foods supposed to bring good luck

hong mu—a fragrant red wood

heimongmong—dark fog

hulihudu—confused

Jyejye—Sister

kai gwa—literally "open the watermelon," also a vulgar term for sexual intercourse

Kuomintang—Chinese Nationalists. Supported by the United States, they wanted the Chinese economy to be capitalist. They were opposed by Communists supported by Russia.

mah jong (also spelled "mah jongg")—a board game

li—distance measuring about 1/3 mile or .5 kilometer

Meimei—little sister

nengkan—total confidence in oneself

ni—a traitor to family ancestors

pai—mah jong tiles

shou—respect for family, including ancestors

Shwo buchulai—"Words cannot come out," expressing frustration

syaujye—Miss, a title

syaumei—a dumpling

Taitai—wife

waigoren—foreigners, especially Caucasians

yang—in Daoist philosophy, the active, masculine force

yin—in Daoist philosophy, the passive, feminine force

zong zi—sticky rice wrapped in lotus leaves

SECTION EIGHT

Bibliography

Quotations from *The Joy Luck Club* are taken from the following edition:

Tan, Amy. *The Joy Luck Club*. New York: Ivy Books, 1989.

Other Sources:

Current Biography Yearbook. Judith Graham, ed. New York: The H. W. Wilson Co., 1992. 559-63.

Heung, Marina. "Daughter-Text/Mother-Text: Matrilineage in Amy Tan's *Joy Luck Club*." *Feminist Studies*. Fall 1993. 597-615.

Miner, Valerie. "The Daughters' Journeys." *The Nation*. April 24, 1989. 566-67.

"Mother with a Past." *Maclean's*. July 15, 1991:47.

Shear, Walter. "Generational Differences and the Diaspora in *The Joy Luck Club*." *Critique*. Spring, 1993. 193-99.

MAXnotes

REA's Literature Study Guide

MAXnotes® are student-friendly. They offer a fresh look at masterpieces of literature, presented in a lively and interesting fashion. **MAXnotes®** offer the essentials of what you should know about the work, including outlines, explanations and discussions of the plot, character lists, analyses, and historical context. **MAXnotes®** are designed to help you think independently about literary works by raising various issues and thought-provoking ideas and questions. Written by literary experts who currently teach the subject, **MAXnotes®** enhance your understanding and enjoyment of the work.

Available **MAXnotes®** include the following:

Absalom, Absalom!	Heart of Darkness	Of Mice and Men
The Aeneid of Virgil	Henry IV, Part I	On the Road
Animal Farm	Henry V	Othello
Antony and Cleopatra	The House on Mango Street	Paradise Lost
As I Lay Dying	Huckleberry Finn	A Passage to India
As You Like It	I Know Why the Caged	Plato's Republic
The Autobiography of	Bird Sings	Portrait of a Lady
Malcolm X	The Iliad	A Portrait of the Artist
The Awakening	Invisible Man	as a Young Man
Beloved	Jane Eyre	Pride and Prejudice
Beowulf	Jazz	A Raisin in the Sun
Billy Budd	The Joy Luck Club	Richard II
The Bluest Eye, A Novel	Jude the Obscure	Romeo and Juliet
Brave New World	Julius Caesar	The Scarlet Letter
The Canterbury Tales	King Lear	Sir Gawain and the
The Catcher in the Rye	Les Misérables	Green Knight
The Color Purple	Lord of the Flies	Slaughterhouse-Five
The Crucible	Macbeth	Song of Solomon
Death in Venice	The Merchant of Venice	The Sound and the Fury
Death of a Salesman	The Metamorphoses of Ovid	The Stranger
The Divine Comedy I: Inferno	The Metamorphosis	The Sun Also Rises
Dubliners	Middlemarch	A Tale of Two Cities
Emma	A Midsummer Night's Dream	Taming of the Shrew
Euripedes' Electra & Medea	Moby-Dick	The Tempest
Frankenstein	Moll Flanders	Tess of the D'Urbervilles
Gone with the Wind	Mrs. Dalloway	Their Eyes Were Watching God
The Grapes of Wrath	Much Ado About Nothing	To Kill a Mockingbird
Great Expectations	My Antonia	To the Lighthouse
The Great Gatsby	Native Son	Twelfth Night
Gulliver's Travels	1984	Uncle Tom's Cabin
Hamlet	The Odyssey	Waiting for Godot
Hard Times	Oedipus Trilogy	Wuthering Heights

RESEARCH & EDUCATION ASSOCIATION
61 Ethel Road W. • Piscataway, New Jersey 08854
Phone: (908) 819-8880

Please send me more information about MAXnotes®.

Name _____

Address _____

City _____ State _____ Zip_____